D0764016

R10

South African

TRIBAL LIFE TODAY

Photography
JEAN MORRIS

Text
BEN LEVITAS

COLLEGE PRESS
Cape Town

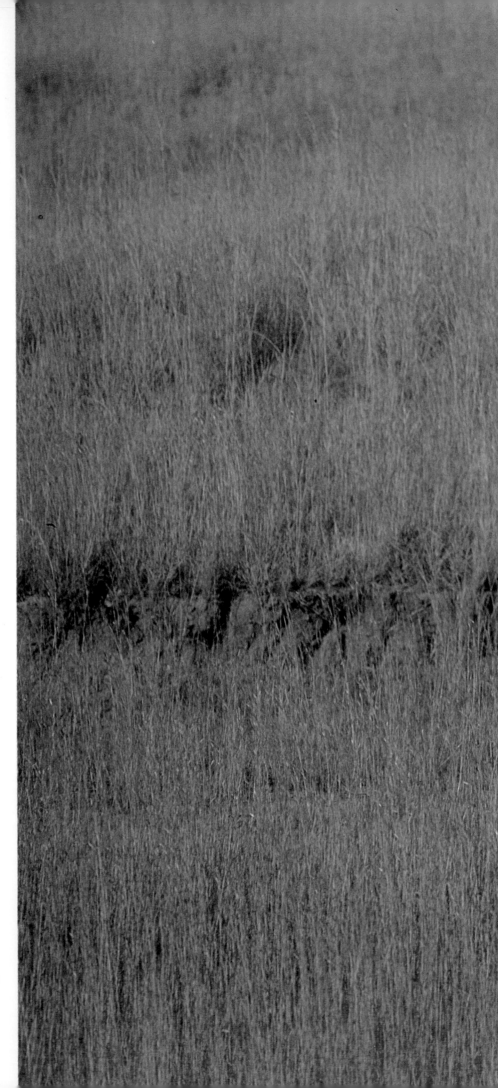

ACKNOWLEDGEMENTS

The photographer would like to acknowledge
the following people for their help and
co-operation in obtaining many of these
photographs:
The former Department of Bantu Affairs
The Department of Information
The Department of Interior
Mrs W Coker
Colin Murray
Graham and Moira Stewart
Norman and Val Yeats
James and Faith Stevenson
Mr C Purvis
James Christie
Mr & Mrs W H Hulett
Miss Angela Hulett
Mr & Mrs G Bridson
Prof John Marais
Mr N Otte
Mr Colenbrander
Mr & Mrs C Pretious
Mrs Diana Gage
Jo and Lynn Farrager
Meshak
Paddy and Maureen O'Brien
Geoff and Eloise Seekings
Colin Ewels
Mr Venter
Mr Barkhuizen
Mr Dietleffs
Hassim Chothia
Mr Geyser
Peter Pennels
Mr & Mrs Dallas Muir
Dr & Mrs Fordyce
Ali and Alma Shepard
Ralph and Auriel Sparg
Mr Daweti
Prof & Mrs Potgieter
Mr Luyt
Simon Manenga
Frieda van der Merwe
Abraham Napo
Mr Laufs
Mr Prozeski
Peter and Elizabeth Walker
Prince Klaas Mahlangu and Princess Orah
Princess Thembi and Richard Ndlovu
Peter van Wyk
Lucas Tshivhase
Rev Dehnte
Sister Goretti
Mr Molepu
Dennis and Margaret French
Chief Mugivhi
Mr & Mrs M Southwood
Chief and Mrs Lencoe
Chieftainess of Gopane
Prof D F Coetzee
Nico and Tersia Hager

and many others too numerous to list.

Published by College Press,
P.O. Box 12088
Mill Street 8010

ISBN 0 620 06338 6

Copyright text Ben Levitas
Copyright photography Jean Morris
Design by Jean Morris and Martin Field
Typesetting by Diatype Setting, Cape Town
Colour separations, printing and binding by
Colorcraft Ltd., Hong Kong

First published in South Africa in 1984
Second impression 1987

All rights reserved. No part of this publication may
be reproduced or transmitted in any form or by
any means without the permission of the publisher
or the copyright holders.

CONTENTS

5 **PREFACE**

7 **HISTORICAL AND CULTURAL BACKGROUND**

13 **HUTS AND HOMESTEADS**

35 **CLOTHES, ORNAMENTATION AND BEADWORK**

63 **FOOD AND EATING HABITS**

75 **ECONOMY**

95 **RELATIONSHIPS**

117 **RELIGION, BELIEFS AND MAGIC**

131 **CEREMONIES AND FESTIVALS**

139 **POLITICAL POWER, ORDER AND JUSTICE**

149 **EDUCATION**

PREFACE

Tribal life today is in a state of flux and of transition. Traditional established ways, based on tribal experience, are no longer adequate or capable of providing satisfactory solutions to problems now being encountered by detribalized people, particularly those who have moved away from their tribal lands. A breakdown of tribal bonds is affecting all the Bantu-speaking people, whether they live in the homelands or in the urban areas. This process of change and of urbanization has dislocated the lifestyle of the ex-tribal person, and left him in a transitory state with two value systems, one tribal, the other western. Such a state of dislocation is not a comfortable one to be in, and widespread social problems manifest themselves and remain endemic until a new balance is reached. Although this state of balance may be eluding many, there are countless others that are adapting well to the virtues and vices of so called "westernization". It is not, however, the intention of this book to highlight some of the unsavoury or unfortunate effects of these changes, although the authors are well aware of their existence. It is our intention merely to record the last remnants of a way of life that is rapidly passing away.

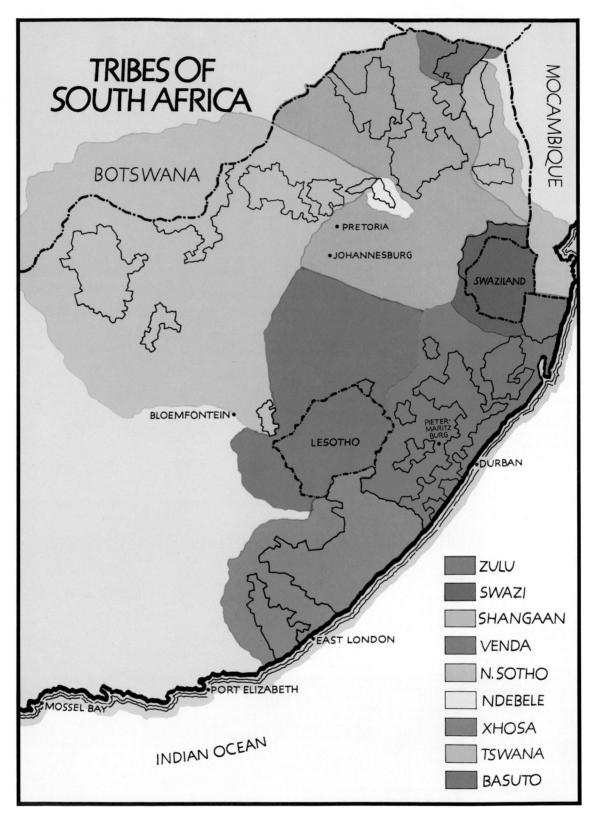

TRIBES OF SOUTH AFRICA

MOCAMBIQUE

BOTSWANA

•PRETORIA

•JOHANNESBURG

SWAZILAND

BLOEMFONTEIN•

LESOTHO

PIETER-
MARITZ-
BURG
•

•DURBAN

•EAST LONDON

•PORT ELIZABETH

MOSSEL BAY

INDIAN OCEAN

ZULU
SWAZI
SHANGAAN
VENDA
N. SOTHO
NDEBELE
XHOSA
TSWANA
BASUTO

Photographs appearing on previous pages:

1 A Xhosa rides leisurely through the Transkeian countryside on horseback.

2 A typical Transkeian scene of white huts dotted on the hillside. They are all built to face the rising sun.

The present day political borders of the homelands do not coincide with traditional tribal boundries, and about half these people live outside the homelands.

HISTORICAL AND CULTURAL BACKGROUND

The photographs in this book are not only of historical interest, they also illustrate a way of life which still survives. Many people continue to live in a traditional tribal manner, particularly in certain rural areas. It is, however, generally true to say that the tribal life-style is rapidly disappearing due to the growth of western influence. These photographs are a testimony to the continuation of tribal values and ways of life. These tribal people are not historical oddities, but represent a highly successful way of life and of adaption to particular environments. Although most of these tribal customs and traditions now occur only in the very remote rural areas of South Africa, they are also occasionally manifested closer to the urban centres. One could, for example, encounter on the outskirts of a town a young initiate, his face smeared with white clay, emerging from some bushes near the road, or even a group of initiates in Soweto. However, because the chances of this happening are rather remote, some of these fast disappearing tribal customs are portrayed here so that they can be remembered.

Tribal life today does not exist anywhere in its pure or undisturbed form. Tribal life, of course, was always changing and being influenced by outside cultures, but today the strongest influence is that of westernization and with it capitalism and industrialization.

Before looking at some specific customs and traditions, it is useful for us to know where the tribal peoples originate and how they come to be living in Southern Africa. The black people of Southern Africa are the descendants of Negroid peoples who moved out of Central Africa about two thousand years ago. The events that triggered off this great migration are not known, but during their journey southwards these Negroids encountered and mixed with many cultures and races, such as the Hamites and the Pygmies.

Before the Negroid peoples moved into Africa south of the equator, the indigenous inhabitants of most of this region were the Khoisan peoples. The word Khoisan is used to refer collectively to the Hottentots, who called themselves Khoi-Khoin, and the Bushmen or San peoples. Although the Bushmen and Hottentots have much in common the latter possessed domesticated animals whereas the Bushmen did not. When the Dutch landed in the Cape the Hottentot people were already living there and they were consequently the first indigenous people that the Dutch encountered. Because the Khoisan people lived in close harmony with their surroundings and possessed a very simple material culture, very little evidence of their widespread former presence has survived. The only physical remains of these indigenous peoples which occur throughout the southern sub-continent are numerous examples of rock paintings, engravings, burial mounds and tidal pools that were used to catch fish. The traditional Khoisan way of life is rapidly disintegrating except amongst the remnants of small scattered bands of bushmen in the inhospitable Kalahari Desert. Place names, such as Griqua, Outeniqua and Namaqua, which are derived from the names of large Hottentot tribes may one day be the only legacy of the Khoisan peoples.

Although now on the verge of extinction these indigenous peoples have continued to have an impact on the nature of South African society. Some of the early Dutch immigrants and other subsequent settlers mixed and integrated with the Hottentots to produce a racially mixed people, the "coloured" people who today number over two and a half million. The Khoisan people also had a marked impact on the nature of the black people with whom they came into contact even before the arrival of the Europeans. This contact produced the Southern African Negroids who characteristically have a lighter skin than the 'true' Negroids of West Africa from whom they originated. Other notable features of some South African blacks inherited from the indigenous Khoisan peoples are a tendency to have so-called "peppercorn" hair, slanted or slit eyes, high cheek bones and enlarged upper thighs and buttocks due to the presence of an additional layer of fat beneath the skin.

On the cultural level an interesting merging of lifestyles occurred between the Khoisan and black peoples. The languages spoken by the black peoples of South Africa have to varying degrees incorporated numerous click sounds which are characteristic of the Khoisan languages. The Xhosa people in particular, because of their more extended period of contact with the Khoisan peoples still speak a language heavily infused with click sounds. The three major click sounds are now denoted by the latin letters x, q and c. Although these clicks imbued their host languages with certain unique qualities, they did not change the fundamental grammatical structures of these languages. All the languages which are spoken by the black people south of the equator form part of a large language family, collectively known as the Bantu languages. Despite being spread over such a wide area, all the Bantu languages show a remarkable degree of structural uniformity. This uniformity has helped linguistic historians to piece together the speed and the routes by which the Bantu speaking people penetrated into the Southern sub-continent.

The vanguard of the southwards movement of Bantu speaking people probably reached the Limpopo by about A.D. 300. Historians refer to these immigrants as 'farmers' because they practiced agriculture and possessed domesticated animals, whereas the indigenous Khoisan population subsisted almost entirely by collecting roots and fruits and by means of hunting. Archaeologists have worked out that these 'farmers' initially penetrated into South Africa along the coastal plain on the eastern coast and then moved inland along the river valleys. Remnants of some of these farming settlements on the central inland plateau have been excavated. Archaeologists have traced some of these settlements back to the fifth century A.D.

Several waves of Bantu settlers from the north were to follow these early farmers. These immigration waves continued well into the eighteenth century. Although all these immigrants spoke Bantu languages, each group possessed and to varying degrees maintained, its own identity, customs and traditions. Simplistically speaking it became possible to divide all the Bantu speaking peoples into two broad groupings: the Nguni and the Sotho. The Nguni now account for about two thirds of the black population of South Africa. They reside along the south eastern coastal plain, being known in Natal as the Zulus, and in the independent territories of the Transkei and Ciskei as the Xhosas and Pondos. The Swazis also form part of the Nguni group although they live further inland. All the Nguni peoples share a similar language and culture. They are, for example, primarily pastoralists, placing great emphasis on their cattle. The fact that agriculture is the preserve of women is indicative of its secondary role in Nguni traditional society. On the other hand the prime position that has been accorded to the cattle herd can be gauged from the extent to which men have made it their exclusive preserve. Women are barred from milking the cows and even from touching the milking utensils. In connection with the cattle herd there are numerous other rules and restrictions that women are required to observe. They are, for example, not allowed to go anywhere near the cattle kraal and this rule is considered to be of particular importance during menstruation, for at this time women are considered to be in an unclean state and therefore a potential danger to the herd.

A Xhosa custom which forbids people who are not clansmen from drinking milk together has some interesting implications. Don't be surprised, for example, when you venture into a Xhosa homestead and partake of their milk if your host concludes that you, his guest, have designs on his daughter, because by drinking milk in his home you are implying that you wish your group and his group to unite into the same clan. This custom consequently makes the men in Xhosa society very careful about where and with whom they drink milk.

The Swazis, Zulu and Xhosa are very large tribes, each with its own language, culture, territory and political structure. The tribe is the largest traditional grouping of people and it includes many clans, each of which is made up of those people who allege that they are descended from a common ancestor. Because oral records are used to trace this line of descent, the identity of the original ancestor is invariably forgotten after about 7 generations. Thereafter he becomes a mythological figure shrouded in mystery. Although his descendants claim to be related to each other, it becomes more and more difficult with each succeeding generation for them to prove that any relationship actually exists. Although no traceable blood relationship may exist between clansmen, Nguni custom assumes that it does exist in that it forbids marriage between members of the same clan. Clansmen recognise that a special bond exists between them which they express by using the clan name whenever it is fitting to bestow special praise, honour or respect on fellow clansmen.

Another group that is of considerable importance is the lineage. This is a smaller group of people over a more limited number of generations, usually from two to four. It differs from a clan in that the identity of the founding ancestor is known and the relationship with him or her can be exactly traced.

The other major grouping of the black people of South Africa are the Sotho. They can broadly be divided into three main groups; the South, West and North Sotho. The combined population of the three Sotho groups is approximately 5 million, which accounts for about one third of the black population of South Africa. Collectively they are referred to as the Ba-Sotho, although this term is often used to refer specifically to the South Sotho. The territory of the South Sotho was formerly known as Basutoland. The West Sotho reside mainly in the independent states of Botswana and Bophuthatswana. Some also reside in the Western Transvaal. The North Sotho are a heterogenous group which include such diverse peoples as the Pedi and the Lovedu. The Lovedu reside on the highveld of the Transvaal, largely within the borders of the homeland Lebowa. The Lovedu people have been distinguished by a succession of legendary "Rain Queens". These queens acquired great prestige during their reigns due to their alleged abilities to produce or withhold rain. Many people and even conquerors like the mighty Mzilikazi, once a commander in Shaka's army, are reputed to have shown her respect and paid tribute to her.

Sotho societies, unlike Nguni societies, are structured around totem groups rather than clans, although the structure of their lineages and extended families is similar to those that are found amongst the Nguni peoples. Clans are not of great consequence amongst the Sotho particularly as they do not forbid marriage between clan members. Sotho tribes are divided up into totem groups each with their own totem, which is usually an animal such as a crocodile (Kwena) or a baboon (Khatla). Although outsiders or immigrants can join a totem group the custom is for membership in a totem group to be passed on from a father to his sons. It is common in the area inhabited by the Sotho to find a particular totem such as the crocodile occurring in tribes widely separated from one another. The myths and rituals once associated with these totemic animals, such as the restrictions on eating, touching or seeing them, have largely died out as a result of the effects of westernization and of detribalization.

There are two other important tribal groups, namely the Venda and Shangaan/Tsonga. For historical reasons they are not included in either the Nguni or Sotho groups. The Venda number about 400 000 people and are centred around the independent territory of Vendaland which is in the extreme North-east corner of the

Transvaal. The Shangaans number about 800 000 but their territory, Gazankulu, which is also in the Transvaal, has not yet attained independence.

Nowadays, with over half of the black people in South Africa living in an urban or semi-urban context, these traditional social groupings have lost much of their relevance and they have consequently ceased to be a major determinant of social behaviour. To an increasing extent more and more black people are being born in urban areas and because they have not experienced a common tribal life they share little in common with blacks who have migrated from tribal areas to the cities. In the latter case the persistent effects of tribal values are still noticeable, particularly in the forms of the organizations and associations that they create. The "home-boy" group, for example, consists of people who come from a similar rural background and who provide support to one another in their new urban environment. With the passing of time all these groupings with links in the rural and tribal past will slowly fade away and be replaced by associations, relationships and organizations that are more appropriate to contemporary circumstances.

The blending of traditional culture with that of the west has resulted in interesting and sometimes bizarre permutations and adaptions. Whatever the form of these traditions and customs, they have shown a remarkable resilience to change and to survive and adapt in their new surroundings. Generally the tendency has been for traditional societies to be swallowed up by western culture, although in South Africa the ways of the past persist largely because they provide an anchor that continues to give meaning to a great number of black people. Their traditions and customs provide these people with a link between the present and the past and a sense of belonging to something enduring in a rapidly changing society. To us the student, the tourist or the lay reader they provide a colourful collage of the diversity of humanity and an alternative way of looking at ourselves.

If we assume that people all over the globe are intrinsically the same, we can learn much from other cultures by looking at the ways in which they solve their problems and how they live their daily lives. Since we are not born with our culture, we have to learn it from our parents, friends, teachers and society. Because we assimilate most of our culture at a very early age, our culture becomes so much a part of ourselves that we take it for granted. We assume things without understanding why, and without realising it our culture makes us see things in a certain way. It distorts our view of how other people do things, especially when their ways differ radically from our accepted norms. These differences invariably lead us to judge people from other cultures by our standards, which often lead us to be critical of the way that others act.

As a result of this tendency, people from a western culture, for example, are quick to look down on people from other cultures who eat with their hands instead of with knives and forks as is the western practice, or who sit on the floor instead of on chairs. But lest we reach such hasty conclusions, let us pause a while before we prejudge or condemn the customs of others.

If you proceed in this cautious manner, you will probably realize that there is nothing preordained or absolutely right about the way you do or have been taught to do certain things. Why, for example, eat with a knife and fork when chopsticks could be equally satisfactory once they have been mastered? Indeed, ones hands could also be perfectly adequate provided that they have been washed first. This way of eating is not really so preposterous, because hands have the advantage of providing the eater with a sensation of touch and of texture which could help to enhance the meal. Another example of how we make biased judgements about the ways of other cultures is our attitude to sitting in chairs. Some customs are based on false premises such as the western attitude to seating. Westerners think it unbecoming of people, especially women, to sit on the floor, despite the fact that there is absolutely no valid reason for such an attitude. In fact, this western attitude has encouraged people to adopt such poor sitting habits and postures that many westerners suffer from chronic back-ache for a great deal of their lives. So, bearing in mind some of these limitations that our culture imposes on us, the reader would be advised to go through these photographs with an open mind and refrain from making hasty or premature judgements.

An old engraving which shows the bridal procession from the homestead of the bride to that of the groom.

11

HUTS AND HOMESTEADS

The huts and homesteads of the tribal people of South Africa vary considerably in design and decoration. The geometric patterns painted on the mud walls of the huts of the Ndebele of the Transvaal are completely different from the straw 'beehive' shaped huts of the Zulu who reside in Natal. The stone walled huts of the Basotho who live on the mountainous plateau of Lesotho, in turn differ greatly from those of other tribes. To what then should these different housing forms be ascribed?

For an answer to this question let us firstly examine the craftsman building the hut and secondly the nature of the building material. Each hut is fashioned around a general pattern which is in accordance with the tribal tradition. No two huts are exactly alike because each is custom-made according to the tastes of its owner. Each hut can rather aptly be said to be 'homemade'. The uniqueness of the building material with which each hut is built is another factor which accounts for this diversity. All building material is entirely natural and nature is always unique in the sense that no two blades of grass or two stones used in constructing huts are exactly alike.

Despite this variety there exists within a specific area a certain degree of homogeneity with regard to designs and styles. Although housing styles have changed over the generations, houses tend to be fashioned largely from the raw materials provided by the local environment. It is therefore not surprising to find many stone huts in Lesotho, where the high mountains provide a large supply of building stone but where trees and even grass are scarce; or huts made from the skins of animals in Namibia where everything except the domesticated herds of small livestock is in short supply. The environment also influences the permanence of settlements. Huts in dry regions are often built to be of a temporary nature and are light so as to enable the group to migrate easily in their search of water and food. Conversely, when the land is fertile and rainfall regular, people can settle down and build permanent homes because their livelihood is more secure.

Apart from the influence of the environment, there are historical and cultural factors which cause housing styles to vary between different tribes. In certain cases both stone and grass may be available as raw materials for building houses and which of these will finally be used in constructing the hut is largely determined by the preferences of each tribe. Not only do the materials that are used vary, but the methods of construction also differ from tribe to tribe. In the latter case there may be differences in the division of labour, or in the times when building is permitted to commence or in the manner of selecting suitable housing sites. Once the structures have been erected the important stage of decorating the external walls commences. One finds both regional and local differences in the decoration of the homesteads. In some tribes the exteriors of homesteads are elaborately decorated with a wide variety of patterns and colours, whereas in other groups the custom is to have no decoration.

Long before the black people came into Southern Africa the bushmen, who were living there, built themselves simple, light and mobile shelters. These huts were generally shaped like a beehive, but because they were not built to last no evidence of them remains today. Some bushmen of course lived in caves; and these cave dwellers have left us with a legacy of beautiful cave paintings.

The first black people to come into Southern Africa from the north probably followed the hut building techniques of the bushmen by building their huts with a round base and a dome in the shape of a beehive. Until the turn of the century most Cape and Natal Nguni peoples and even the South Sotho built beehive shaped huts. Afterwards the rondavel which retained the circular ground plan of the beehive huts but had a conical shaped roof instead of a dome, became so popular that many people have falsely assumed it to be the indigenous form of the hut. The rondavel hut is generally circular (although, despite its name, it can also be rectangular) with clay walls and a thatched conical roof. The roof is generally built separately from the hut

Previous page:
3 Zulu homesteads on the hillside in the lower Drakensberg region of Natal.

4

5

4 The first stage in the construction of a Zulu "beehive" hut is to form a framework by bending and securing saplings with string.

5 "Beehive" shaped huts in a Zulu kraal.

and only fixed into position once the walls are completed. Amongst Tsonga people the roof rests on two concentric circular walls with the outer one built lower than the internal one. The outer wall is either left open, with the supporting staves providing an airy veranda along the circumference of the hut, or the area between the supports can be closed up which allows the space between the two walls to be used for storage.

Doorways, particularly into the traditional beehive huts, are small and so low that people are required to bend down to enter. A small door made from a frame of saplings interwoven with grass is pulled across the entrance and secured to the main hut at night. In addition to the aforementioned, it is customary to have a small wind screen near the door. Nowadays doorways in the urban areas are much larger and some closely resemble those of western houses. In the centre of the traditional hut directly in front of the doorway there is usually a fireplace. In traditional societies who were very conscious of sex differences, it was customary to divide the hut into a left hand side where only women were allowed to sleep and a right hand side where only men could sleep. As western notions of egalitarianism have spread, such customs have been modified.

In Zulu huts the back part is considered to be the most important section. Strangers are strictly forbidden to enter this section of the hut and it is the preserve of the homestead head and the woman of the hut alone. Sleeping in this part of the hut is taboo, for it is here that spirits are believed to live. Because of this belief, offerings are made to the ancestral spirits in this sacred part of the hut. Considering that this section is generally out of bounds to all outsiders, it serves a useful function as a storeroom, particularly for the more valued possessions.

The floors of most huts are made from a mixture of clay and cow dung. These ingredients are beaten with stones into a smooth paste and smeared smoothly over the floor by hand. In the past this process was often repeated several times a week until the floor assumed a smooth, almost marble-like, shining appearance. Nowadays it is more common to encounter floors with a matt or cork-like texture.

Most of the furnishings inside the hut are either stored in the sacred place at the back, or on shelves or on racks built into the walls or tied to ropes connected to the rafters. Skins or grass mats serve as beds and these are rolled up each morning and fastened to the rafters.

Apart from mats which are used as seating, the furnishings of huts and homesteads are very simple. Before the arrival of Europeans it was customary to use wooden neck rests, some of which were intricately carved. Some museums display an amazing variety of these wooden neck rests. These have subsequently been replaced by soft pillows except amongst those Zulu women who still wear their elaborate circular hairstyles. Western-style furniture such as chairs and tables were almost unknown before contact was made with early missionaries and tradesmen, but certain tribal groups started making very simple European-style furniture shortly after coming into contact with them. The Tswana for example, have for a long time now been making a folding chair with thong seats. Amongst the Venda and Sotho groups it is customary to build solid clay bench seats as extensions from the supporting clay walls of huts rather than have movable chairs or benches.

As is the case with people throughout the world, people tend to live together in communities of various sizes. Similarly in a tribal setting huts seldom occur individually but are grouped into homesteads. Generally amongst the Nguni people these homesteads or 'kraals' as they are commonly referred to, are based on an individual family. These families are large polygamous families who are comprised of the homestead head, his wives and all their children. Occasionally a married son may stay on in the kraal of his father, but this is usually only a temporary arrangement because it is widely believed that "two bulls cannot live in the same kraal",

6   7

6 and 7   Dry grass is firmly tied with ropes of plaited grass over the sapling framework. Women can often be seen cutting grass and carrying it home in large bundles on their heads.

8   A little Zulu girl sweeps the entrance of the hut.

9   Because of the shape of the traditional hairstyles, Zulu women sleep on wooden head rests. They lie on mats woven from reeds which are rolled out on the floor of the hut at night.

8   9

meaning that the potential for conflict between two household heads in one household is great.

Whereas the Nguni homesteads are often widely separated from each other, the homesteads of the Sotho people are arranged more closely together into villages. Some of these villages, especially as they occur amongst the Tswana, can grow into very large settlements of over 25 000 people. The dryness of the country which compels people to settle near water sources and the flat nature of the landscape can account for this phenomenon amongst the Tswana. Due to the dryness and flatness of the country, villages are located near water and also serve a defensive function due to the absence of natural obstacles, such as caves or mountain fortresses.

In the hilly parts of the country which are inhabited mainly by the Nguni people and the Venda, huts are built halfway up the slopes on the hillsides so that they face the rising sun and avoid the effects of the cold air which collects along the valleys. The huts of the Nguni people are traditionally arranged in a circular form. The hut of the homestead chief is customarily located at the highest level of the village, from where it looks over the cattle enclosure which is the social and spiritual centre of the homestead.

The huts in Zulu homesteads are customarily grouped in the form of a circle around a cattle enclosure. Very large homesteads belonging to important chiefs could contain a large number of huts to house all the wives of the chief, their children and their guests. The huts in these cases were usually arranged in two concentric circles. The pattern amongst the Xhosa was traditionally in the form of a semi-circle, although nowadays huts are more often built next to each other in straight rows.

The doorway of each hut faces towards the focal point of the homestead, namely the cattle kraal. Each wife has her own hut and often has separate huts for cooking, entertaining and for storage. The hut of the chief wife is of special importance and is consequently in a central spot, with the huts of the other wives arranged around it according to their status. The homestead head rotates from hut to hut and it is the responsibility of the wife that he is with to cook and care for him. While he is with a certain wife in her hut, none of the other wives are permitted to visit him, even if there is no one in the hut. Older boys and girls are usually provided with their own huts, as are guests.

The above description of traditional tribal housing is of course becoming less accurate with every passing day. With over 50 per cent of the black population currently living in urban areas, western housing styles, methods of construction, materials and value systems, have exerted a strong and irreversable influence on the nature of housing for blacks. Even in rural areas where the pull of tribal values is still apparent, the influence of western housing styles and materials will have altered the nature of the huts and homesteads drastically from the traditional.

10 Zulu children inside a traditional "beehive" hut. The concentric-shaped framework can clearly be seen. From the roof hang skeins of plaited grass ropes used for securing the thatch onto the framework of the hut.

11 The horns of cattle on the thatched roof above the doorway of a Zulu hut signify that it is the hut of a chief.

12 A Pedi kraal built at the foot of a rocky outcrop in the Northern Transvaal. These kraals usually have a front courtyard for visitors and a rear courtyard for family use. The terra-cotta walls around the kraal are sometimes decorated in geometric patterns.

12

13 Decorative fences around a Zulu kraal in the foothills of the Drakensberg mountains.

13

14 An Ndebele village where traditionally the mud walls are painted in colourful geometric patterns by the women. The walls are made of mud and cow-dung.

14

15 Originally natural pigments were used for paint but nowadays acrylic paints are common. Traditionally Ndebele huts had thatched roofs but the modern trend is to use corrugated iron instead.

15

16 A beautifully made Swazi "beehive" hut made of bent saplings and covered with dry grass.

17 This Mapoch woman stands proudly outside the house which she has painted. The interior walls of the house are painted in exactly the same manner.

18 Clothes and sleeping mats are stored on poles under the roof inside a Swazi hut.

19 A grandmother and children in front of a different style of hut in southern Swaziland.

20

21

20 A Tswana house, typical of the Taung region in the north-eastern Cape. The walls are not painted and are the colour of the earth of this area. Patterns are scraped into the mud before it dries.

21 Thatched terra-cotta walled huts of the Tswana, in Botswana.

22 A hut for storing mealies within a Tswana kraal is raised above the ground to allow the air to circulate.

23 Basotho huts made of local stone near Matsieng. The thatched roof extends over a porchway painted in natural terra-cotta.

24 ▲

25

24 Xhosa rondavels or conical huts on the road to the Wild Coast in the Transkei.

25 An old man returning to his village in Lesotho. During the winter months the huts are covered with snow and ice.

26 Grain baskets and rolled-up sleeping mats are suspended from the roof of a Xhosa hut when not in use.

27 During the winter months the mountainous regions of Lesotho are covered in snow, and remote villages can be completely cut off, causing food shortages.

28

28 An unusual mud wall around a Venda hut in the southern
Sibasa region of Vendaland.

29 A Venda village where the huts are clustered together.

30 A Shangaan village which shows the traditional huts with covered
verandahs, formed by poles under the circumference of the roofs.

29

31 The very earliest style of Shangaan hut with a thatched roof reaching right down to the ground. This style is rare nowadays. Nearby is a small chicken hut raised off the ground on poles to keep predators away.

32 A hut door, neatly made from saplings which are bound together with goatskin thongs. This door slides across the low doorway of a Shangaan hut at night, and is secured with a pole from the inside.

33 Although the Abantwane are an offshoot of the colourful Ndebele, their huts are surprisingly monotone in colour.

34 The outer walls and entrance to a Pedi house are ornately patterned in two tones of mud. The cow-dung floor of the courtyard is also patterned in the same way; patterns are made by hand while the mud and cow-dung is still soft and wet.

35 A particularly decorative hut in Swaziland, though not typical of the region, resembling more closely the style of huts found in Lesotho

36 A different style and pattern of hut decoration in the Orange Free State, made by an imaginative Sotho woman.

37 Mass housing in Soweto consisting of small brick houses.

38 An example of a more westernized hut in the Transkei.

CLOTHING, ORNAMENTATION & BEADWORK

Unless you have actually spent time living amongst people who still adhere to a tribal way of life you will probably be under the impression that tribesmen are people who wear little, if any, clothing at all. It may therefore come as a surprise to you to learn of the importance attached to clothing amongst tribal people.

In this book our discussion of clothing will be limited to style, fashion, ornamentation, beadwork and colour. Even though some tribal people appear to go naked for most of their lives we should pause a while to consider "nakedness" which is of course a relative concept; what makes one person feel naked does not have the same effect on another. It should be realized that because tribal people do not share the same inhibitions as do westerners, the absence of a certain item of clothing considered to be vital by a westerner, would not even be missed by a tribesperson, and vice versa. For example, a tribeswoman without a small earring or chain of beads may feel less dressed than if her breasts were completely exposed.

Thus, in order to understand the dress of a society, one should look at the meaning or value that the wearer attaches to his clothing rather than retain one's own culturally biased perception of his dress. Clothes often acquire symbolic values, especially when they are associated with certain religious, social or ceremonial occasions.

In western societies, conservative or modest clothing is usually the appropriate style of dress for visits to churches and other religious occasions. In tribal societies religious regalia often sports a rather different style. The naked body is permissable in many religious ceremonies, although it usually has to be elaborately prepared and decorated before the ceremony commences. The body is prepared for religious occasions, firstly by means of a purification ceremony and then by a strengthening process.

Purification ceremonies take many forms and do not all involve dress or ornamentation. Sometimes the part of an animal which is closely associated with a purification function in the animals body, such as the bladder, is worn by the person who needs to be purified. A young person after menstruation may, for example, be required to adorn her hair with a goat's bladder, so that she may be purified from her unclean state. When she marries, the bride may again be required to wear the bladder of a goat that has been ritually slaughtered to ensure that her forthcoming marriage will be blessed by her ancestors. Apprentice diviners or witchdoctors also pass through a ritual whereby they are required to adorn their bodies with the bladders of animals which have been ritually sacrificed during their training.

Strengthening ceremonies usually require special medicines which are carefully collected and prepared by herbalists. These medicines are often poured over or rubbed into the skins of the people that require strengthening. The tribal kings are anointed with animal fats in much the same way as the biblical kings were anointed with oil. Kings also exercise certain privileges in that only they are entitled to wear the skins or parts of certain animals. The right to wear the leopard skin is an example of such a privilege for only the king and certain chiefs are entitled to wear the skins or parts of the leopard. In rare cases, even chiefs are excluded from wearing certain parts of an animal as in the case of a necklace of lions' claws reserved exclusively for the Zulu king.

The dress of kings is also associated with long feathers e.g. that of the ostrich or the blue crane or the red feathers of the lourie bird which are worn by the Swazi

39 An intricately patterned beaded cape with long beaded tassles, worn by a young Zulu woman in the Drakensberg region of Natal.

royal family. The tails and furs of various animals, such as blue monkeys and genets are sometimes also worn by royalty. Apart from these few items which to the westerner may seem trivial, tribal kings in their day-to-day style of dress, look very similar to the ordinary tribesmen. Tribal kings do not wear ornate crowns or elaborate clothing and do not live in large palaces as do many of the western kings. Nowadays tribal chiefs and kings wear western dress except for certain traditional occasions.

One group of tribespeople who tend to have a very decorative style of dress are the diviners, witchdoctors and herbalists. Whether the diviners are men or women, their hairstyles tend to be very striking. Depending on the tribal group, their hair is often plaited or twirled into very tight coils which are then rubbed with butter, globules of soap or fat. Some tribes use ochre to give their hair a red lustre. Multicoloured beads, shells, coins or almost anything are tied to the hair to add a final touch. Zulu diviners, for example, twirl black cotton around strands of hair into which small groups of white or coloured beads are inserted. This process lengthens the hair which hangs in long braids over the shoulders and down the back.

Diviners can usually be distinguished from other tribesmen by the long cross-over strips of skins and beads worn across their chests, and by the amulets or small containers which are often beaded and which are carried around their necks or waists. These amulets are similar to the western doctor's bag in that they contain many of the most commonly required medicines, mostly ground roots and herbs. Other necessary aspects of the diviner's attire are a switch made from the hair of the tail of a wildebees, a snuff box which contains the snuff that helps the diviner to clear his head in order to correctly divine the cause of the misfortune, and mainly amongst the Sotho tribes, a container for the divining bones, kept sometimes in the skin of a small animal such as a civet cat.

Witches in western society are characterised in literature by a particular type of dress. This is not the case in tribal society, where witches or sorcerers can be ordinary folk. Sometimes these ordinary folk are not even aware of the fact that they are causing harm because their powers are said to be unconscious. Because witches are so similar to the ordinary people, a specialist, the diviner, needs to be called upon to 'smell' them out, and to identify them.

The dress of the ordinary people varies tremendously from tribe to tribe and even within the same tribe there are differences. Where beads are widely used, the pattern and colours show tremendous variation. In the days of old before trade was started with Europe and China, beads were made from natural products such as ostrich eggshells, seashells and from an enormous variety of seeds and the peels of dried vegetables. Trade opened up a whole new assortment of beads, initially made out of glass and later out of plastic, and offered the skilled craftsmen undreamed-of opportunities to make intricate patterns with bright, strong colours.

A similar transformation occurred in the use of textiles and fabrics. The Arabs in particular introduced superb cloth into Africa that was not only superior to the locally manufactured products but also more easily and rapidly produced. When this improved imported cloth was added to the artistic flair and workmanship of the tribespeople, this marriage produced beautiful designs and colourful patterns.

Before the widespread use of linen and cloth, other natural products such as skins and grasses provided the main raw materials that were used for making clothes. In this book you can see various examples of the pleated cowskin skirts worn by Zulu women, or of the animal skins and pelts that are worn by men.

It is of great interest to note that dress is very closely associated with the various stages of growth in a tribal person's life cycle. Most infants wear little or no clothing. Amongst the Ndebele, young children are given a bead necklace or a single strand of white beads to wear around their waists even before they are clothed. Young children wear a minimum of clothing, usually only a small loin-cloth or an apron of skins attached to a waistband. In most tribes the transition from infancy to childhood is marked by a ceremony. Amongst the Zulu for example, the children have their ears pierced to mark this transition. According to their custom this helps to improve the children's hearing and understanding. Pieces of a twig or of a corn-stalk are inserted into their earlobes. These earplugs are increased in size as the child grows older until the outer earlobes stretch around an earpiece that can be as large as the top of a teacup. Among other tribes the small loin-cloths of the girls are replaced by larger string or thong aprons as the child grows older. Beads are often attached to the ends of these aprons, although occasionally the whole apron is encrusted with beadwork.

Traditionally in all societies, the marriage ceremony marks the beginning of the most significant period in a person's life, and it is accompanied by a great number of changes in clothing and ornamentation. Married women usually wear a blanket or cape that covers their breasts. Marriage also always marks a change in hairstyle. Some tribes, such as the Ndebele shave the girl's head completely, whereas others such as the Venda shave around the sides of the head leaving a tuft at the top of the head. The Zulu on the other hand encourage their girls to lengthen their hair before marriage and to arrange it into a small knot before stretching it over the traditional circular frame. When Zulu men marry they are permitted to wear a permanent headring around the circumference of the top of their heads. Many years ago the custom was to wear a waxed headband into which the hair was incorporated.

To enhance the period of pregnancy, Zulu girls wear a maternity apron made from skin of a buck killed by her husband during her pregnancy. The buckskin is said to impart grace and strength to the unborn child. Sometimes special charms, such as fertility dolls, are worn or made to ensure a successful and productive marriage.

After marriage, girls are not supposed to dress in a style that will attract the attention of other men. As a consequence fewer beads tend to be worn. Immediately after marriage, the new wife is subjected to a whole body of *hlonipa* rules, whereby she is expected to show respect to her husband's family. At this stage the wife is expected to wear certain clothes, such as a veil of beads or a handkerchief, which can only be removed once she is fully accepted into her husband's family.

Clothing and beadwork convey important messages particularly before and at the time of marriage. Certain beads for example indicate that a girl is engaged, whereas the so called Swazi and Zulu bead 'love-letters' can convey a whole range of romantic meanings and messages. These are exchanged between lovers, generally by means of their friends. While courting, much time is set aside to attend to external appearances. The young men at this time only don the best animal skins and they are also adorned by beautiful feathers and a small courting shield. During the wedding-procession girls often carry artefacts or wear clothes that symbolise their purity. To symbolise their virginity, Zulu maidens carry an assegaai, Ndebele maidens wear white beads, whereas girls from other tribes carry spears or wear the skin of a particular animal.

After studying the photographs you will most certainly gain an appreciation of the graciousness, beauty and a variety of clothing that is worn in tribal societies. The degree of harmony between body decoration, dress, beads, hairstyles and colour is always apparent. Unfortunately, due to the increased price of the beads obtained at trading stores, the intricacy of the work and the length of time required to make tribal clothing, fewer and fewer examples of these clothing styles are found. The influence of tribal styles however, continues to determine the dress of large sections of the black community. The bright colours which are so popular amongst the black consumers nowadays and the style with which they are worn bear testimony to the enduring appeal and influence of tribal clothing.

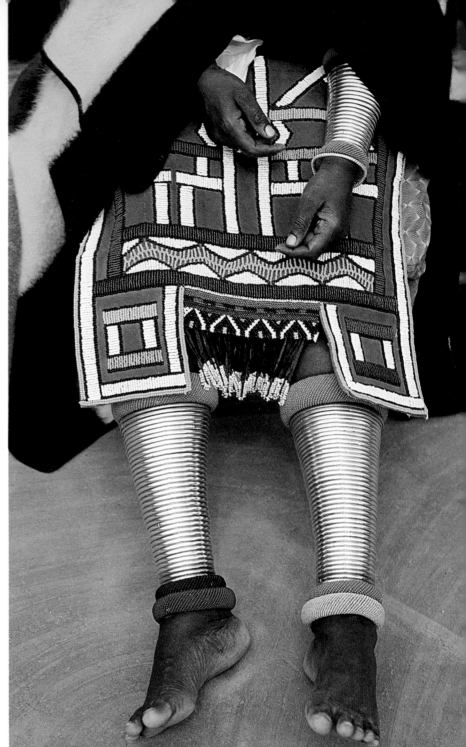

40▲   41▼

42▲   43▼

40 The brass neck-rings of an Ndebele woman which signify her married status are often surrounded by a beaded neck-hoop.

41 An Ndebele woman wears the long beaded strips of a marriage headdress which extends from head to foot.

42 Significant to the Ndebele is the marriage apron, traditionally made of leather, on to which a pattern of beads is sewn. The brass rings on her legs are another mark of marriage. These, together with those around her neck and arms, may only be removed if her husband dies.

43 An intricate border of beadwork decorates the lower edge of an Ndebele blanket.

44 A young married Ndebele woman adorned with the brass neck bands of marriage which she wears night and day.

45 An Ndebele mother wearing the enormous traditional beaded neck-hoop and colourful wide-striped blanket.

46 Additional decoration is often added to the large beaded hoops. The insides of the hoops are made of coils of dried grass, around which the beads are woven.

44

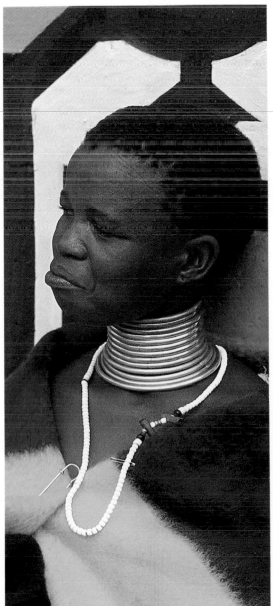

45▲ **46▼**

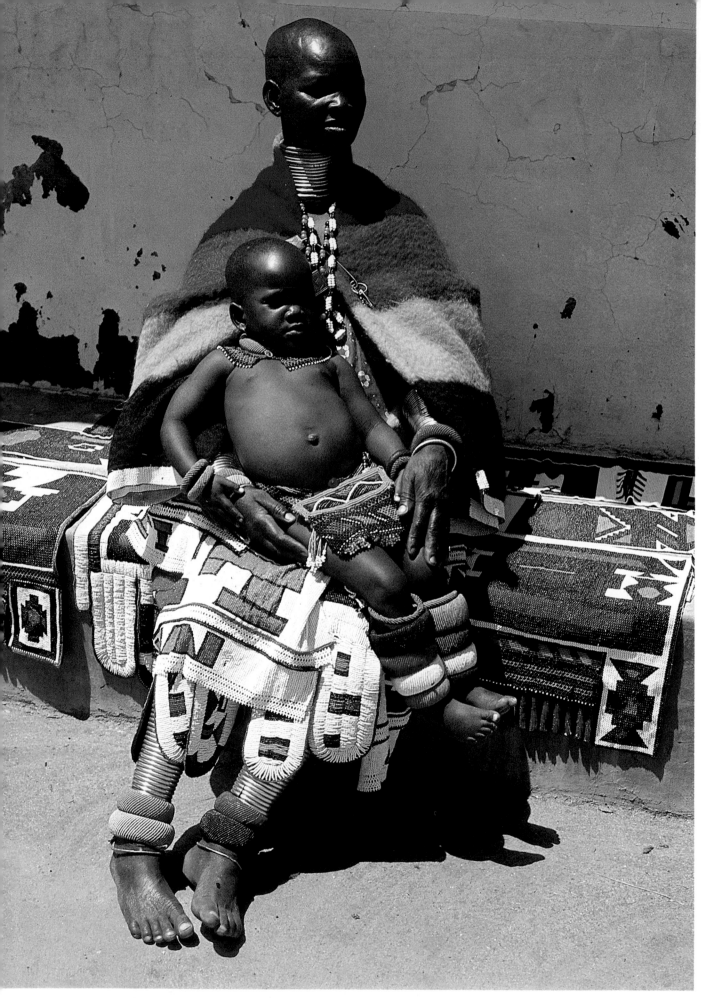

47 An Ndebele mother and her child seated on the wall outside her house, on which are displayed a selection of marriage aprons. The scalloped type of marriage apron which she is wearing is of an older traditional style.

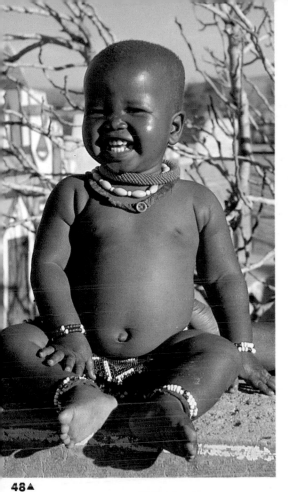

48▲   49▲   50▼

51

48 An Ndebele baby wearing her first single strand of beads.

49 A group of Ndebele children. The boys wear small leather loin-cloths and the girls have small square beaded aprons and beaded leg and arm bands. These decorations are now only worn on special occasions.

50 An unmarried Ndebele girl shows her beaded fertility doll to a young child.

51 An Ndebele child dressed in beaded arm and waist hoops also displays a traditional bead headdress.

53▲

54

52 A young boy wearing a traditionally patterned Basotho blanket.

53 A Basotho herdboy in a harlequin patterned blanket.

54 A young Basotho herdboy sticks a feather in his hair for decoration.

52

57 Zulu hairstyle, seen in the Drakensberg region.

58 Detail of a recent trend in Zulu beadwork.

59 The traditional pleated cowskin skirt worn by a married Zulu woman. The skin is softened by rubbing fat into it with a stone and blackening it with soot from cooking pots.

55 and **56** Bands of beadwork decorate the headdress of a married Zulu woman. It is made from hair woven with string and ochre.

55

56

57

58

59

60

62

63

61

64

65

A variety of Zulu hairstyles: 67▶

60 The hair is stretched over a light wooden frame and ochred. Her earlobes have been enlarged since childhood to now accommodate very large discs.

61 Hair woven with red string has additional decorations for this wedding guest.

62 An elongated version of the "flower pot" hairstyle (**63**) made from ochre and string, as seen in early engravings of the Zulu.

64 Hair stretched sideways and decorated on the ends with studs, and with a beaded "catherine wheel" of horse hair in the centre.

65 Strands of hair elongated and stiffened with horse hair. Herbal medicines are carried in her necklace.

66 Shiny plaits of horse hair artificially lengthen the hair of this unmarried girl.

67 This pregnant Zulu woman is wearing a bead decorated apron of the skin of an antelope killed by her husband, which she believes will keep the unborn child safe from harm.

66

68▲

69

70

71

72

68 A Zulu child with bead decorations in her hair, wearing stiff bead necklaces of this region.

69 A young Zulu with an artificially elongated strand of hair and horse hair to which beads and an old army button have been attached.

70 Two young Zulu boys wearing traditional animal skin aprons and bead necklaces.

71 A little Zulu girl at a trading store in the Keates Drift area.

72 A Zulu baby girl in bright beaded skirt, in contrast to the dry surrounding countryside.

73 A Zulu dressed for a wedding, wearing broad bands of colourful beadwork.

74 Numerous bands of beadwork decorate the blanket of this young Zulu woman seen near Winterton in the Drakensberg. She also wears the traditional cowskin pleated skirt.

75 Bright red dresses and scarves are traditionally worn by the Zulu women of the lower Drakensberg in Natal.

73▲　　74▼

75▼

76 and 77 Xhosa youths dressed for a party.

78 The characteristic long pipe is traditionally smoked by women in the Transkei.

79 Traditional ochred material skirts worn by Xhosa children.

80 A Xhosa woman with ochred face.

81 Wood and string necklace typically worn by Xhosa women.

82 A Pondo girl, her legs heavy with wire bracelets.

83 A Pondo woman with beaded marriage head-coil, her "lengthened" hair bound with ochred cotton and decorated with beads.

76▲ ▼78

79

80▲ 82▼   81▲ 83▼

84▲

85▲

86

84-86 Hairstyles of unmarried Bhaca women from the Richmond area in Natal.

87 Married Bhaca women wear a characteristic decorated knob on their heads and often wear many layers of skirts.

87

88

88 Young Xhosa girls dressed for a Sunday afternoon gathering of young people on a hillside near the Wild Coast in the Transkei. Their heads are covered with heavy woollen scarves carefully folded in a "turban-like" manner.

89 They wear cotton skirts with rows of tucking and masses of bead bracelets adorn their ankles.

89

90 Two of the many wives of a Shangaan homestead head-man, wearing dresses of brightly coloured material knotted on the shoulders. These are worn over short traditional pleated skirts.

91 Colourfully dressed Shangaans chat by the wayside.

92 The traditional multi-pleated Shangaan skirt made from a length of striped cotton material several metres long. It is sometimes beaded along one edge for decoration and to give weight. This is especially effective in the "hip-flicking" traditional dance.

92

◄90   91▲   ▼93   ▼94

95

93 Venda women traditionally wear striped salempore material with additional braid sewn on. Unique to the Venda are the chalk stiffened white pompons.

94 and **95** Very young Tswana children wear a beaded apron and later one of string.

96 Xhosa youth dressed for a party.

97 Pondo girl with characteristic hairstyle and scarification marks on her face.

98 Bracelets in Xhosa society are a status symbol and they are made from wire bought at trading stores. Her rings are from the tops of cold drink tins.

99 The particularly wide style of folding the heavy woollen material on the head is characteristic of the Engcobo district of the Transkei.

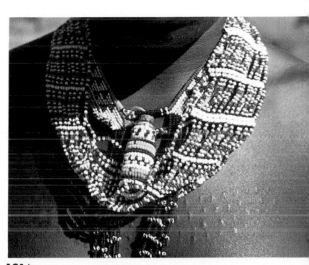

100 Two Ciskeian girls dressed in their traditional finery.

101 In addition to the many strands of beads this Xhosa girl has a pattern of raised bumps on her skin.

102 Two Xhosa girls on the banks of a river, after scrubbing their colourful bracelets and washing their hair in readiness for a party.

100▲ 102▼   101▲

103 Swazi men wearing the traditional scarves knotted on one shoulder and skin or cotton skirts. They raise their sticks or "knobkerries" as a form of greeting.

104 A group of young boys dressed in green leaves dancing by the roadside in the north of Swaziland.

105 Two Swazis share a joke. The hair of the man on the left is covered in a mud pack of ground leaves and ash to lighten the hair, this custom being peculiar to the Swazi. The red feathers signify that they are members of the royal family and the two bead patterned squares of the necklace are the traditional "love-letters" worn by Swazi men and women.

106 A Swazi mother-to-be wears a goatskin apron for the well-being of the forthcoming child. The "beehive" hairstyle with the cord of white string at the hair-line is characteristic of the Swazi.

107

108

107 Posing with a battle-axe, the traditional Swazi fighting weapon.

108 Swazi women love colour and often wear many brightly coloured scarves.

109 A Shangaan girl displays the many metal bracelets on her arm. The scarification markings on her face, now considered a sign of beauty, date back to the times of the Arab slave traders. In the days of slave trading, girls were scarred to spoil their beauty.

110 A little Shangaan girl wearing a scarf of cotton with simple beaded motifs.

111 Brightly dressed Shangaan women wearing wide beaded necklaces and heavy metal bracelets.

109▲   111▼

110 ▲

112

113

114▲   115▲

116

112 An Abantwane woman with beaded neck hoops and arm bracelets. The black cotton headscarf is folded in a characteristic Abantwane manner.

113 In the same kraal these Abantwane women display their best dress, which is modelled after the style of the dresses of early missionaries and has now become the accepted form of dress.

114 Under the beaded headpiece of a married Pondo woman, the hair is twisted with black cotton to give it the appearance of strands of long hair. The sides are clipped down, and in this case the hair behind her head is bound with pink cotton and the ends decorated with beads.

115 Pedi women arriving at a trading store wearing the highly favoured bright pink head-scarves. The necklace of huge beads is also typical.

116 The head scarves worn low over the face as protection against the bright sun are a feature of the Pedi.

117 A Lovedu woman wears a black skirt edged with a braided band of beadwork and bright coloured cotton scarves over her shoulders.

117

118 In the early morning a young Basotho child blows the flame to kindle the fire under the cooking pot containing the mealie-meal porridge for breakfast.

FOOD AND EATING HABITS

The large herds of cattle are a tribal man's most valued possessions. Cattle are not only the ultimate symbol of wealth but are also the central focus of the tribes's social, religious and political life.

Seen in this light it is not surprising to understand why cattle are not slaughtered for food. Only very special occasions such as weddings and sacrifices to the ancestors can justify the slaughter of cattle. However, once the cattle have been sacrificed or killed for these important occasions, all parts of the animal are carefully cut up and fully utilized.

As most tribal people prefer not to obtain meat from their cattle, they seek it instead from their herds of domesticated goats, sheep and fowls. Meat does not however feature as a regular part of a tribal person's diet, which is mainly made up of mealie-meal or porridge. Meat is considered to be a luxury that is greatly sought after, and consumed in large amounts whenever it is available, such as at weddings and initiation celebrations.

Traditionally most of the meat eaten is obtained from hunting, not from the domesticated herds. Because hunting tends to be unpredictable and as hunts are organised sporadically, the meat supply from this source tends to vary greatly. Although tribesmen have their preferences, they tend to eat almost any meat, except when taboos restrict them from eating certain animals, e.g. the totem animals or fish which many groups consider to be unclean. Predators of the wild, including birds of prey, also tend to be avoided. Meat is also obtained from wild birds, termites, locusts, flying ants, caterpillars and a variety of other worms. Indeed the Mopani worm is considered to be a great delicacy by certain groups such as the Tswana and the Shangaan. As a rule women are forbidden to consume the meat of animals which have aborted or died during birth, lest they suffer a similar affliction. Although chicken is considered to be the proper meat for women to eat, they are not encouraged to eat eggs lest they become filled with lust. This taboo is applied particularly to adolescent girls and to girls on the threshold of marriage. Men on the other hand, consider eggs to be a great delicacy and they attach particular value to the aphrodisical properties.

The main staple of all the Bantu-speaking tribes is maize, which ironically is an alien plant introduced into Africa originally from America via Europe. The next most important staple crop is millet or sorghum ('Kafir corn'). As this is an indigenous crop, it was the basic staple crop before maize was introduced. Wheat is of no consequence in the traditional diet. 'Kafir corn' is prized, because it is the basic raw material for the traditional beer. Apart from water and milk, beer is the only other traditional beverage. It is less alcoholic than western beer, but because it is consumed in large quantities it also achieves the desired results. Because the beer contains much solid material it is more than merely a highly nutritious beverage, it is also a food. Other less popular varieties of beer are made from maize, marula fruit, the leaves of prickly pear and from a variety of the palm tree. Beer is not only consumed for its inibriating qualities but its consumption plays an important part in the social life of the community. It is the most important commodity at all ceremonies and feasts; it is the accepted means of settling quarrels and disputes, of showering hospitality on a guest, of according tribute to a chief and of cementing friendships. Beer is an important ingredient in offerings to win the favour of the ancestors and to thank them for good harvests, rain and good fortune. Beer is also used as a means of payment for work done and as an incentive to get work done.

Both 'Kafir corn' and maize are ground down, either on a stone or pounded by heavy poles in a wooden container or sometimes taken to a local trading store to a mechanical grinder. It is then mixed with boiling water to form a thick porridge. Maize is also prepared on the cob by either roasting or boiling it.

Other vegetables are cultivated according to the terrain and the different climatic conditions of the widespread tribal regions. Sugar cane, beans, peas, groundnuts, sweet potatoes, melons, and pumpkins are either dried or stored to be used in winter. Vegetable stews are often prepared and herbs and salt are used for flavouring. Insects, particularly locusts, when crushed and ground into a fine powder, provide a much relished flavouring agent for food and are very nutritious.

Everywhere milk from cattle and goats is a staple drink of great importance. The milk is generally permitted to curdle and thicken into a form known as 'amasi' by the Zulu. It can be eaten with almost any other food or by itself. Fresh milk is rarely drunk by adults but is given to children.

There are a great number of taboos regulating the drinking, eating and procurement of milk. Many of these stem from the fact that cattle are usually considered to be the exclusive domain of men. Women are not usually allowed to milk the cattle or even to touch the milking utensils. Amongst the Nguni, women are also forbidden to drink milk with non-clansmen. Because newly-wed brides come from an outside clan, they are initially barred from drinking milk in their husbands' home. Men also have to exercise caution over who they drink milk with, for should a man drink milk in the home of a non-clansman, this will be interpreted as a sign that he wishes the two clans to unite by marrying a girl from the other clan.

It is customary to have two meals a day, one in the mid-morning at about 11.00 a.m. and another in the evening. Because the men and boys usually leave for the fields before the first meal is ready, they scrounge around for leftovers from the meal of the previous evening or obtain whatever they can in the countryside. Consequently, this meal is mainly for the women of the homestead. Because the men return in the evening from the fields ravenous from lack of food, the evening meal is the more substantial. It usually contains a thick gravy and hopefully some meat served together with the thick porridge.

Although the evening meal is a family or communal affair, the participants are divided up strictly into age groups. There are small separate groups of women, older men, younger men and children around the eating area. As each group eats apart from the others, they each have their own communal serving bowl from which each person in that group can fill his own bowl. Eating and the distribution of food occurs strictly in order of rank, with regard to age and sex. The young children often receive only the scraps and sometimes have to be satisfied with licking clean the plates of the adults. Traditionally food is eaten with fingers while sitting on the ground, but nowadays it is often served at a table.

The detribalized people no longer live in such close harmony with the bounty of nature, eating the fruit of each season. The food they now eat closely resembles what the Europeans eat. Each homestead no longer prepares its own beer as the days of self-sufficiency are past. Food is now processed in factories and obtained from stores. The enormous size of the black consumer market will certainly ensure that they make an important contribution to the tastes and preferences of South African consumers, as they will largely dictate what will be produced.

119 In the special hut for cooking, a Venda woman rubs the stirring stick between the palms of her hands.

122▲ 124▼

123

120 A group of women in a Venda village drink from dried calabashes which are used as drinking utensils.

121 Whilst her baby sleeps on her back, a Venda women inspects the ground mealie-meal.

122 A Venda woman tosses the corn to separate the chaff from the grain.

123 With a heavy stamping pole the grain is pounded into flour.

124 Wearing traditional dress, a Venda woman cooks a meal outside her hut.

125 A Lovedu housewife selects pumpkin leaves to cook in the pot at the side of her.

126 A Swazi mother grinding corn. Stones for grinding are carefully chosen as they perform an essential part in food preparation.

127 Zulu children gather around the big ▶ black cooking pots in a corner of the kraal which is set aside for cooking.

128 Swazi women stir the evening meal. ▶

129▲

130

129 A Xhosa woman removing the mealie kernels from the husk.

130 A Xhosa woman, with her baby sleeping peacefully on her back, grinds mealies with a.smooth stone on a grinding-stone.

131

132 Pedi women cooking for their husbands, who are selling their cattle at a cattle auction in the Northern Transvaal.

◄**131** At some trading stores in the Transkei, women can take their mealies to be ground by machine. Due to the great distances between stores, the women often have to walk for many kilometres carrying heavy sacks of grain on their heads.

133 Tswana women preparing beer for a wedding celebration. The beer is made from fermenting mealies and is a staple food and an integral part of all celebrations.

134 A Shangaan woman wearing a traditional pleated skirt serves beer from a calabash to her visitors.

135 A Shangaan woman kneeling at the cooking pot stirring the mealie-meal.

136 Shangaan housewives stamping mealies with extremely heavy poles in alternating rhythmic beats.

137 A young Pedi woman with a scarf which almost covers her face for protection against the hot sun, carries home a container of water drawn from a river many kilometres from home. Leaves are placed on the surface of the water to avoid evaporation by the sun and to keep the water cool.

135

136▼

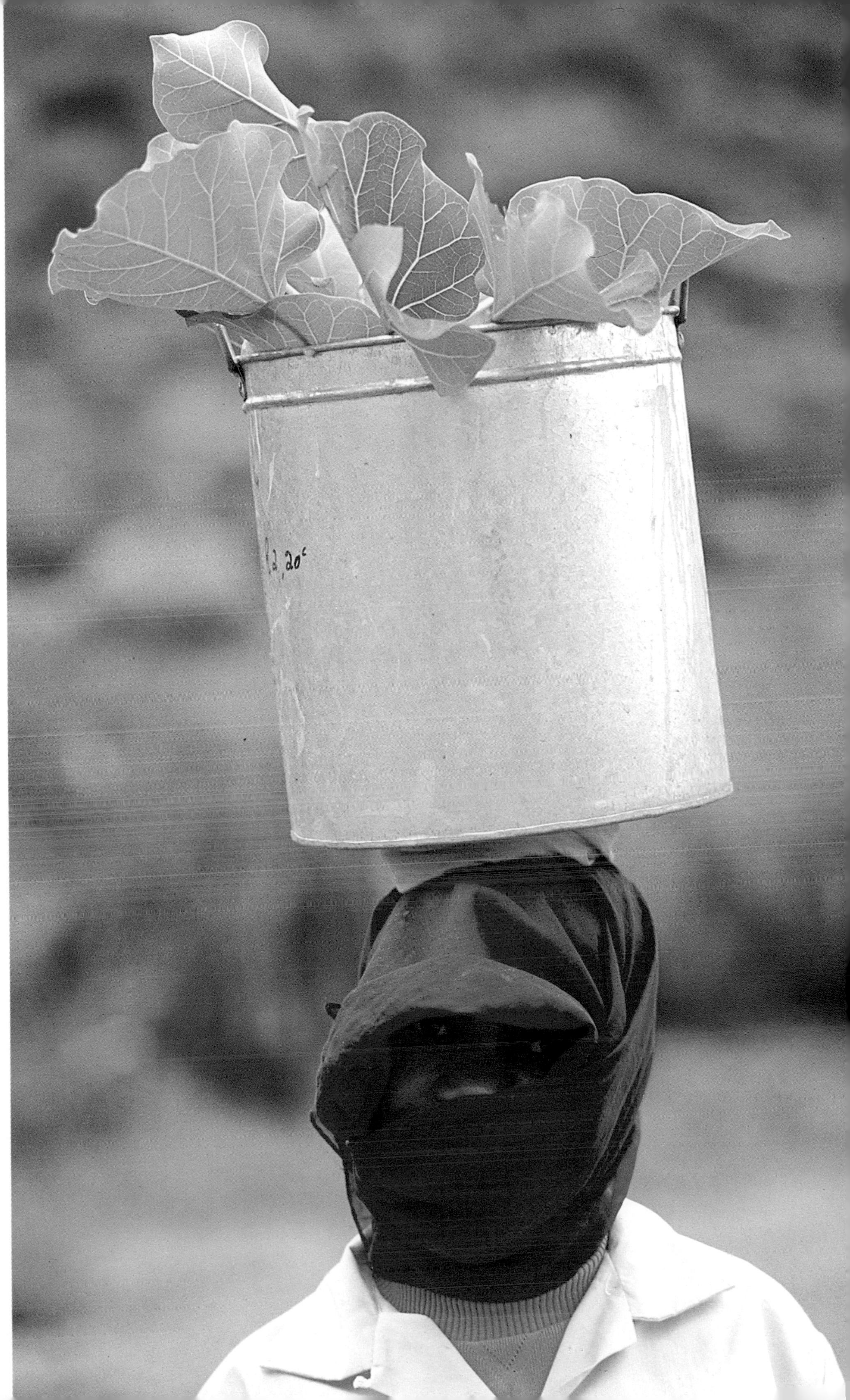

ECONOMY

Previous page:

138 An ox-drawn plough, still widely used in the homelands.

139 A young Basotho woman selling woven grass hats and reed sweeping-brushes intricately bound on the tops. These items are handmade in peoples' homes and are bought by local people and tourists. Handicrafts form an important source of income to the people of Lesotho, as the country is poor and there is little industry.

140 The Basotho grass hat is a well known symbol of the country and appears on the national flag. Each hat varies in design according to the individual who makes it, but they basically have the same pointed shape with decorative loops at the top.

141 Women selling vegetables at the market in Maseru, the capital of Lesotho. Women predominate in these fresh-produce markets, particularly as they are mainly responsible for the growing of vegetables. This income supplements the family income, as many of the men are away on contracts working on the mines in South Africa.

139

The economy is the system that provides for man's needs and wants. All people have the same needs, such as warmth, shelter, security, love, food and drink, but societies differ when it comes to satisfying their wants. In western society wants are defined as being unlimited for when a want is satisfied it is merely replaced with another. Western economies create wants all the time by means of advertising and by changing fashions or by offering a wide variety of products for the same purpose.

Although most of the black people living in South Africa have now been drawn into a western type of economy there is a great section of this population which lives at a subsistence level. A subsistence economy is one that caters only for the most basic needs of people such as housing and food, leaving nothing over. In these economies there is no accumulation of wealth, no saving for the future and no investment. People live from day to day and from hand to mouth, because coping with the present is so all-consuming a task that no thoughts can be given to the future.

Although tribal societies are generally classified as subsistence economies this is only partially true. It is true that most tribesmen are concerned with life on a day-to-day basis, but for some there is sufficient excess available for the occurence of wealth. The chief is the wealthiest man because he controls the largest herds, because he allocates the land to his people, because he receives tribute and taxes from his people and because his people can be required to work for him. But the ordinary tribesman also has wealth, which is usually measured according to the number of cattle or livestock or hoes for agriculture that he possesses.

Most of the Bantu-speaking people in Southern Africa pursue mixed economic activities; such as agriculture, hunting, trading and animal husbandry or pastoralism. Particular groups generally prefer one particular kind of economic pursuit such as pastoralism above all others. Most of the Nguni groups prefer pastoralism and this preference is reflected in the great importance that they place on the herd. The fact that only men are allowed contact with the herd and that women are relegated to agricultural work, is illustrative of the importance that they accord to their livestock.

Wealth is determined by the size of a man's herd and after his own family, a man's cattle are his dearest possession. Unfortunately it is the number of cattle and not the quality of the cattle that is considered to be important and this has serious consequences, namely overstocking of lands which is a big problem particularly in the homelands where overpopulation is making heavy demands on the limited land available.

A man's cattle are so important to him that he does not slaughter them except on certain special religious and social occasions. For meat a tribesperson will turn to the other domesticated small livestock such as goats or lambs or more probably to chickens. Sometimes hunts for wild animals are organized both for the excitement of the occasion and for the meat which is the prize of the event. Cattle of course are used by the man to settle the bride price or Lobola, with which he acquires his wife. Lobola is not only a payment to the bride's family for the loss of her services, but much more. It serves to legalize the marriage and legitimize the offspring from it. Because Lobola cattle are obtained from the relatives of the groom, it also serves to unite the kin of the two families and bestows the right of the groom's family to play an active part in the lives of the newly-weds.

The milk from the cattle and goats provides the main staple food, curdled milk, on which the people are largely dependant. In an earlier chapter we told of how they eat this together with all their other foods.

The division of labour between men who look after the herds and women who do the agricultural work has already been alluded to. The women also do the housework, fetch the water from the river, carry firewood for many kilometres in enormous bundles on their heads, make the fire, and prepare the food. Men are only called upon to help with the agricultural work at certain stages, particularly when new fields are being prepared which requires trees to be cut and chopped down. On these occasions the men organize themselves into working parties and expect to be well catered for by the host, particularly with beer.

Within the traditional economies there are a range of specialists providing various artefacts which requires special skills that are highly prized. The iron smelter and blacksmith possess the secrets of converting the raw iron ore into finished products which are required by the society, such as spears, hoes and other implements. With the spread of imported methods of extraction and of manufacture from the industrialized economies of the west, these crafts have almost entirely died out. Other specialists include the potters, the weavers, the beadmakers, the carvers and so many others.

All these products have for centuries been exchanged and traded. Certain tribes or groups of people, such as the Lemba and the Tsonga, have acquired reputations for being intermediaries or specialists in plying goods between these different peoples. The gold from Zimbabwe, the copper from Phalaborwa and the ivory from the Transvaal filtered through these intermediaries and down the trading channels to people from China and Arabia that called on East African ports long before the arrival of the first Europeans.

The traditional tribal economy has now largely been swallowed up by the burgeoning South African economy. The tribal homelands make a very small contribution to the Gross Domestic Product of South Africa. As a result of the economic underdevelopment of the homelands there are many factors propelling tribal people off their lands such as the scarcity of good land, droughts, pests, outdated technology, and an absence of men in the workforce due to migratory labour. There are, on the other hand, many equally strong attracting forces which tend to pull these people into the industrialized and urbanized centres in South Africa, such as an abundance of work opportunities, and the appeal of the glamour of city life. As a result of these opposing forces the migrant labour system has come into being. Almost half the male population of the tribal homelands leave their families behind in the tribal areas with the good intention of finding work so that they can make enough money to send back to them. Although this does occur to a large degree, many men are less fortunate because they cannot find work or even if they do succeed, they may not be able to save enough to send anything home. This widespread phenomenon, that is men leaving their homelands to seek work in the cities has also resulted in widespread social problems and has had a particularly adverse effect on the tribal way of life especially because of the central part which men play in tribal society and family life.

142

142 A simply constructed wooden sleigh is still used in the rural areas of the Transkei as a means of transportation for heavy goods, such as the sacks of flour seen here.

143 A Pondo woman who has been hoeing all morning in the fields with her baby on her back. Babies are carried on their mothers' backs while they go about their daily activities; working in the fields or at home, or walking long distances carrying water or firewood. On her head she carries a typical basket made of grass with an indentation underneath to allow it to sit easily on her head.

144 A well made ox-drawn sleigh with built-up sides of woven saplings. The oxen here are led by a young Xhosa girl wearing an ochred blanket.

145

145 Having bought a roughly-made wooden coffin and other goods at a trading store in the Transkei, local shoppers help this Xhosa woman raise and balance it on her head to carry it home, which might be a considerable distance on rough roads.

146 Masses of wire and beaded bracelets cover the arms of a Xhosa woman purchasing a new blanket to wear. As a blanket is an important and expensive item of clothing, it is a major purchase and much thought goes into selecting one.

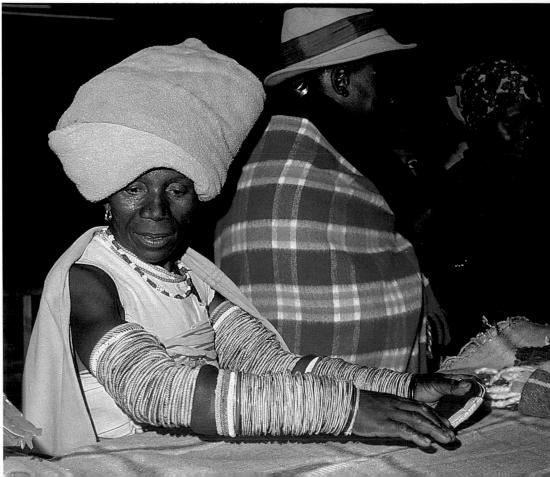

146

147 A Zulu woman selecting a skirt in a trading store in the Keates Drift area. Her ochred hair set well back on her head is the characteristic style of this region, as are the pompons hanging down her back.

148 A group of Xhosa women sitting outside a trading store discussing their purchases. A visit to a trading store is also a social event, as it is the place where news and gossip are exchanged.

149

150

151

149 A vegetable market in Mtubatuba, KwaZulu.

150 A Zulu handcrafts market on the Natal south coast.

151 A roadside pottery market at Mtunzini, along the Natal north coast.

152 A Zulu woman making a huge circular grass mat.

153 A Zulu woman starts to make a grass basket.

152

153

154

154 A Swazi woman at a shopping centre in Mbabane, the capital of Swaziland.

155 A young Swazi wife in the reed-fenced courtyard of her home making an oval grass mat.

156 Scything and gathering grass for handcrafts and for covering huts is a womans' occupation, as portrayed by this brightly dressed Swazi woman.

156

155▼

157 The large handicraft market and adjoining fruit and vegetable market in Mbabane, Swaziland, are centres of attraction to locals and tourists alike.

158 Two small boys in northern Swaziland look after a roadside display of well-carved wooden bowls.

159 A small Xhosa herdboy on the Wild Coast of the Transkei. From 3 years of age onwards, young boys start looking after the herds.

160 A group of young Xhosa herdboys.

161 A goat kraal. Enclosures of large sticks and thornbushes are made at the homesteads to keep the animals safe at night.

162 A team of donkeys pull a primitive plough in KwaZulu.

163 Drying tobacco leaves around a Venda homestead.

164 Mats of ethnic designs woven from raw wool, made at a Catholic mission in Vendaland. The sale of these mats provide the women weavers with much needed money.

165 A Venda woman carrying a bunch of bananas.

166 A young Basotho boy watches his father shearing a sheep. The wool is used to make thick rugs and carpets, a large number of which are exported.

160

161▼

162▼

163▲

164▲

165▲   166▼

◄167 Donkey carts are a characteristic feature of the Tswana, and are used to transport people over the large distances between farms in Botswana.

168 Small Zulu boys loading a sack of grain onto a horse's back.

168

169

169 Herdboys bringing donkeys back to the kraal before nightfall. When animals graze near to the homestead they are brought back each night to be enclosed in kraals to keep them safe from predators, and taken out again early in the morning by herdboys.

170 A small herdboy driving cattle to a lake to drink, in Vendaland.

170

171▲

173▲

172

171 & **172** Chopping firewood and carrying it home on their head in huge bundles is a daily task for the African rural woman.

173 A Swazi basket-maker carrying a batch of cane baskets to sell at a market.

174 An Ndebele woman hoes the ground at the side of her house.

174

175

177▼

175 Shangaan women laying sisal fibres over racks to dry.

176 A Shangaan woman making a section for a large sisal mat.

177 Cutting sisal in the plantation.

176

178 Tswana boys driving a donkey-drawn water cart during the dry winter period.

179 Tanning leather is an important craft of the Tswana.

180 A variety of handmade utensils of the Shangaan.

181 A Shangaan craftsman hews a piece of wood for the lid of a utensil.

182 In traditional style this woman washes clothes by rubbing them with a stone on a rock in the river.

183 Two Shangaan girls conversing after fetching water from a water pump.

184 A Lovedu woman hoes mealies in the garden adjoining her hut.

180▼   **181**

RELATIONSHIPS

In all societies, whether they be western or tribal, the relationships formed between members of a family and those between young lovers are the most important ones that are experienced. These relationships are complex because they consist of many facets which are able to arouse numerable responses or feelings such as love, hate, dependency, need, insecurity, loyalty and trust. Other less complex relationships are formed between the members of society and between them and their rulers. These relationships are simpler because they are more structured and because the roles and relative power positions of each party is more clearly delineated.

The polygamous family is a striking social institution in traditional tribal societies, particularly because of its rareness in contemporary western societies. Polygamous families are characteristically comprised of a man, his wives and their children. In rare cases, variants of this type of marriage could occur, when a woman marries another woman as found amongst the Lovedu people. Very wealthy women may even marry several men, although this is very rare. Due to the spread of western values and the expense involved in providing for such large families, these complex families have largely been eliminated. They do however, survive in the independant black states of Southern Africa particularly amongst royalty and the wealthy.

Not all the wives in a polygamous family are equals. Amongst the wealthy and important male citizens it is an important tribal custom to marry a principal or main wife. This wife must be selected from the correct social status or even from a certain group or clan. Because it can take a long time to find the main wife, such important men are permitted to take another wife or wives in the meantime. Should a man therefore proceed with marriage, the son of the first wife will not necessarily be the heir to his father's estate. Tribal custom requires this good fortune to be granted only to the son of the recognized chief wife.

It could transpire that the chief wife may only be found and married when her husband is already advanced in age. By the time this marriage is ready to produce a son, the children from the first wife may already be grown up. This situation can obviously lead to problems in practice, particularly if the husband were to die suddenly. In these situations squabbles often arise between the children and between their mothers as to who should be the heir to their father's estate.

Generally however, the members of this large family co-exist peacefully and happily. Because age and sex are the main determinants of status, the oldest male in the household is the dominant person. The women are hard working and their main task is to take care of their family and husband. The wives generally get on well together and respect each other. A new wife is considered to be a very junior member of the household. She is obliged to show respect not only to all other wives but to all the members of the husband's family as well. This respect, or *hlonipa* as the custom is called amongst the Nguni peoples, is expressed in a variety of ways. In its most extreme form it forbids the new wife from looking directly at or talking to certain people. In fact it even requires that she avoid certain people altogether. In some cases the young bride is even expected to avoid uttering sounds similar to those of the names of her husband's relatives. This taboo results in the usage of a special *hlonipa* language which the young bride must master.

These taboos play a very important practical social role in that they provide an acceptable safety valve to relationships that are often characterized by tension. All over the world the most common conflict relationship is one between a bride and her mother-in-law. It is not surprising therefore to find that many of the *hlonipa*

Previous page:

◄ **185** A Swazi wedding procession coming up from the valley below, where the bride and guests gathered to dress themselves for the occasion. The bride wears a red woollen veil and a new blanket, and the procession is headed by her sister who carries wedding gifts of rolled sleeping mats and neck-rests for the new hut. They proceed to the kraal of the bridegroom's family where the celebration takes place, having had a feast at the house of the bride's family the night before.

customs are centred around this relationship. There is another strange relationship that characteristically occurs between social equals, which is known as the 'joking' relationship. People bearing this relationship with one another are required to tease, joke and poke fun at each other. Because this is the expected form of behaviour by the society, none of what is said is taken too personally by the parties involved. This relationship also serves to provide a safe outlet for tensions which may arise between two people who may be competing with one another.

Within these large families every child obviously has many brothers and sisters. Despite the fact that they all come from different mothers, thet all call one another brother or sister and so form one large family. Although there is not the same social emphasis placed on the identity of the biological mother as occurs in western society, the children are of course aware of her identity. The children also have many grandfathers or big-fathers, as they are literally called, and grandmothers, or big-mothers. Again, they don't distinguish between their real grandparents and those of the other children. Instead all the children respect and love all the grandparents. In tribal societies as is the case almost universally, the relationship between grandparents and grandchildren is typically of an easygoing and relaxed nature. This may be because of the fact that the grandparents are usually not responsible for disciplining the grandchildren and they consequently tend to be very tolerant of their behaviour particularly their excesses. As a result of this tolerance the grandparents are often called upon by their grandchildren to intercede on their behalf with their 'unreasonable' parents.

The children in such a large family naturally have a great number of aunts and uncles. Apart from the relatives of the husband they generally treat them all alike and call them by the same term. The North Sotho present an interesting example of how social bonds take precedence over sexual differences. A North Sotho man, for example, addresses all his wives' relatives as "mother", whether they be male or female, and a wife addresses all her husband's relatives as "father", irrespective of their sex. The important differentiating criterion is determined only on the basis of age as older people are designated "big" mother or father as the case may be.

These large families may appear to be strange to a westerner and many misunderstandings have arisen between westerners and tribally oriented people because of the westerners' failure to come to terms with the nature of a kinship group. Misunderstandings can often occur in companies or in other work settings when a tribally orientated person requests permission to go on leave several times during a year to attend either a funeral or a wedding of a brother or sister or aunt or uncle. After many such weddings and funerals the company's personnel director may begin to suspect that he is being taken advantage of, because in terms of his own social horizon he cannot conceive of any person having such a large family.

The relationship between a mother and her infant child is generally very close, both physically and emotionally. The child is tied tightly on to her back and stays there while the mother goes about her daily activities. However, it has been observed amongst certain Swazi groups that parents treat their very young infants rather coldly. For example they don't name them and refrain from much physical contact with them during the first three months of the child's life. The high infant mortality rates that are endemic in tribal peoples may partially account for the unwillingness of Swazi parents to invest much emotional content into such a tenuous life. Apart from this exceptional case the child's first major physical separation from its mother occurs with weaning, which is usually at about three years of age.

While the children grow up they are divided into age groups. Initially these groups are sexually mixed and informal play groups. After about seven years of age they become formalized into sexually separate groups. Within these groups the children are equals, although each group does elect a leader who is usually someone noted for his physical prowess amongst the boys or for her dancing or singing ability amongst the girls. The members of these groups are socially inferior to everyone who is older than they are and they must obey instructions and show respect to all elders.

Before a person can be accepted into a tribe as a fully matured and responsible member, they are required to undergo an initiation ceremony. This ceremony usually occurs during the period of adolescence and it marks in both symbolic and physical development the transition from childhood to adulthood. Because of the importance of this period and because of the hardships that must be endured by the initiates, many close and lasting bonds of friendship and of comaraderie, very similar perhaps to the bonds of friendship formed between soldiers in a war, are formed.

After initiation or sometimes just before, a period of courting is common. During this period, the thoughts of boys and girls are preoccupied with love and they spend much time grooming themselves. Grooming practices vary but invariably they require the young lovers to cut or oil their hair, to paint or tatoo their bodies and to decorate themselves with beads or skins or colourful feathers. During this carefree time there is much dancing and merrymaking and there are many opportunities to encounter the opposite sex. Although many close relationships are formed during this time, not all of these will result in marriage. Although there is considerable scope for physical contact to take place between lovers, to make a girl pregnant brings shame and disgrace to both families and therefore special care is taken to avoid this occuring.

Nowadays, as more and more people are moving into the cities, the close relationships that bind members of a family and tribe to each other are being loosened. The need for closely interrelated groups is still apparent and is being expressed in the emergence of a variety of new relationships and groups. One notable example of such a group is the voluntary association. In the cities people are being drawn together on a voluntary basis to co-operate in pursuance of a wide variety of goals. Voluntary associations are operating to help their members who are in need; to provide medical help; or even to organize social and sporting events.

The finely woven network of social relationships that bound the tribe closely together have now largely been untied by westernization. The migrant labour system which has accompanied the spread of westernization has largely destroyed the fabric of traditional social bonds. Polygamous families are rare, while illegitimate offsprings and absentee parents, particularly fathers, are now commonplace. Children are often reared by grandparents, which has introduced a multitude of disciplinary problems.

186

187 The mother of the bridegroom, holding grass brushes, dances with a row of Swazi women. They wear the traditional red scarves and pleated cowskin skirts, with dried pods around their ankles which rattle as they dance.

188 A headman wearing traditional cotton skirt and buckskin, chats with the brightly-dressed unmarried girls during the celebration. The red feathers in the hair denote that they are members of the royal family.

186 The procession passes through the cattle kraal, the most revered part of the homestead.

189 The master of ceremonies throughout the day's celebration, proudly poses with "knobkerrie" raised and a large cowskin shield. The cotton skirt with monkey-skin apron, strands of cowtails on his arms, fur and bead necklaces are a fine example of the Swazi traditional dress.

191 The Swazi bride, wearing a bright red woollen veil and inflated goat bladder from a goat ritually slaughtered the night before at the feast held at her parents homestead. She also wears a scarf with traditional patterns, a black cowskin skirt and "love-letter" beads.

191

190 The unmarried girls, spurred on by a headman, come up in a group from the valley below.

192▲

193

192 A Pedi bride dressed in all her finery, seated inside the hut with her attendants.

193 The chieftainess of the area attending a Pedi wedding. She wears a full length leather skirt decorated with beads.

194 Women and men sit in separate groups at weddings. The red pleated smocks are a shortened version of a fashion that they adopted from early missionaries.

194

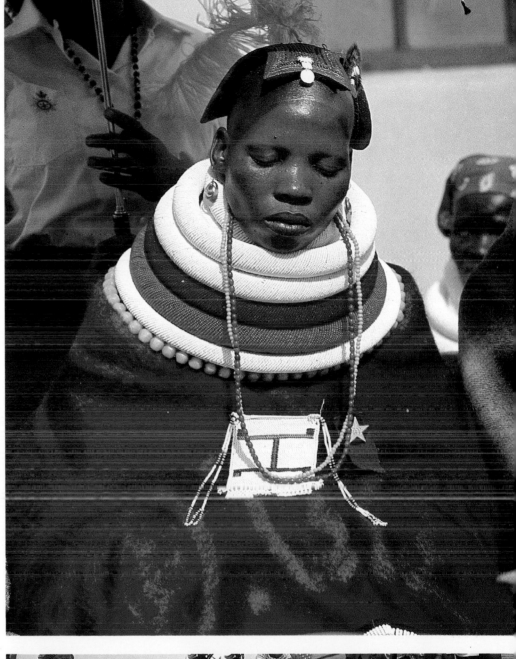

195 An Abantwane bride, shielded from the sun by a black umbrella, must retain a solemn expression during the ceremony as she is leaving her own family to live with another. This is a serious occasion, and if she smiled it would bring disgrace on both families. The marriage hairstyle has taken many hours to create. The sides of her head have been shaved leaving a top knot above, which is mixed with mealie-meal and soot from the undersides of cooking pots and formed into a helmet shape by female relatives. Before it has completely set it is decorated with patterns made by a corn stalk, decorated with beads and topped with an ostrich plume. The scalp underneath is painted with fat and dye. Should this special marriage headdress break or crack during the wedding celebration it would bring bad luck on the marriage.

196 Setting out the wedding gifts at the Abantwane wedding.

197▲   198▲   199▼

197 Traditional and western styled guests arriving at a royal Zulu wedding.

198 The bride, Zulu princess and sister of King Goodwill Zwelithini, arrives by car at the bridegroom's kraal in the royal retinue from the royal home in Nongoma. She is in traditional dress, wearing a leopardskin and wisps of cowtails on her arms, and has a bridal veil of green wool.

199 The King spurs on the dancers on the hillside in the late afternoon.

200▲

201▲

202

203

200 The same evening, after the traditional celebration all afternoon, the bride wears a western-style wedding dress and tiara to attend a reception and dance in a hotel, which lasted until the early hours of the morning.

201 The wedding cake at the reception.

202 The following morning, back at the bridegroom's kraal, the praise singers sing their praises to the couple.

203 One of the praise singers colourfully adorned.

204▲ ▼205 206▼

204 The four best oxen, which had been inspected by the King on his arrival at the kraal, are slaughtered and their meat hung on the fence of the cattle kraal prior to the wedding feast.

205 One of the wedding guests wearing a colourful assortment of beadwork.

206 A lively Zulu dancer stamps his feet to the rhythmic clapping.

207▲

207 After the wedding feast a procession of girls carry the wedding presents to a place on the hillside where they will be presented to the bride.

208 While the men dance in a separate group in the valley below, the bride, now in Edwardian dress and surrounded by a huge circle of women, accepts the presents to the accompaniment of much excitement and ululating. Her two sisters announce from whom each present comes, while the bride notes it in her book.

208

209 A Xhosa woman with her contented baby on her back. For most of the first year or more of a baby's life, it is carried around in this manner, which establishes a very close relationship between them. On her shoulder she also carries a bag in which she keeps her long pipe and tobacco.

210 A Bahlaloga woman sits with her children outside a trading store.

211 A Tswana grandmother looks adoringly at her little grandchild. Nowadays young children are cared for by their grandmothers when their mothers work.

209▲   ▼210   211▼

▲212　　　213▲

212 Traditionally, very young children are cared for by older girls, which teaches them the responsibility of childcare from an early age.

213 Babies and very young Tswana children wear small beaded front skirts.

214 A Venda grandmother bathes her grandchild in the courtyard outside her hut.

214

215 Xhosa men dressed-up to attend a Sunday afternoon party on the hillside. The numerous strands of beads, made by their girlfriends, are only worn on special occasions.

215

216

216 The young men and women at the party dressed in their Sunday best.

217 Pondo youths, complete with axes and sticks for self defence, prepare to go to a party to drink beer and meet the girls.

218 Young unmarried Xhosa girls grooming themselves to meet the boys at an afternoon party.

▼217   218▼

219▲

220

219 Guests line up at a Zulu engagement to give their presents to the engaged girl, who is seated on the ground wearing a cowskin cape and money notes in her hair.

220 At the wedding of a Zulu apprentice diviner the bride, on the extreme right, dances in a group with her two attendants. She wears an inflated goat bladder on her head, of a goat ritually slaughtered for the occasion. They are wearing heavy cowskin pleated skirts, masses of wire bracelets and broad bands of beadwork.

221 Late in the afternoon towards the end of the wedding ceremony, the bride and her attendants, with the bridegroom in the background, continue dancing for many hours. She now has money notes in her headdress, which are gifts from her guests. Bands of sweets and toffees are also worn around their heads for decoration.

221

222▲

223

224▼

222 Guests at a Xhosa girl's engagement party. Food for the festivities is being prepared by the women.

223 Goat meat and mealie meal is cooked in the three-legged iron pots.

224 The engagement presents are displayed for all to see.

226

225 Froth spills over a full barrel of beer. The highly nutritious beer made from fermenting mealies is consumed in large quantities at such celebrations.

226 Women drinking from a large can of beer which is passed around amongst themselves.

227 Women guests sitting around and chatting. Women and men drink in separate groups on such occasions.

225

227▼

228▲

228 Male relatives, with raised sticks in greeting, arrive at a Swazi engagement. They are dressed in their best traditional clothes.

229 At a certain part of the ceremony, the engaged girl, seated on the ground, has fat rubbed into her skin by her grandmother.

229

230▲

231

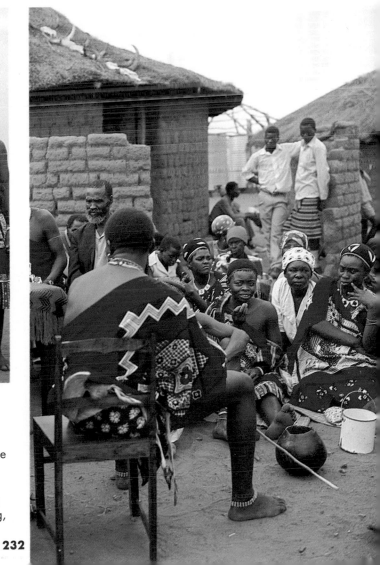

230 Around the engaged girl stand a circle of her relatives, showing their grief at her leaving the family, by a display of "mock" crying.

231 The newly engaged girl on the extreme right poses at the end of the ceremony with her husband-to-be and his two existing wives.

232 After the ceremony the chief, seated at the table on the left next to the engaged man, presides over the present-giving, while the newly engaged girl sits on the ground with the other women.

232

RELIGION, BELIEFS AND MAGIC

Religion plays an important part in all societies because it provides accepted answers to the spiritual needs of people. Religion explains how and why we are here, where we go to from here; how we should act during our lives and why we should do so. It also provides explanations for occurrences which neither science nor experience can explain. In western societies science has become a religion to large sections of the population in that it provides explanations for many phenomena which previously fell exclusively within the sphere of religion. These people regard the things that science cannot explain as superstition or as a chance or freak phenomenon.

Although the black people of Southern Africa have embraced Christianity on a very large scale, certain elements of their traditional religions still survive. As the lives of many black people are in a state of flux, many of these survivals co-exist side by side with Christianity. In such a transitional period people look to the traditions of the past to guide them through the confusion of the present. Unfortunately while the people are changing their lifestyles neither the solutions of the past nor those of westernization are able to offer satisfaction.

This situation is well exemplified when it comes to seeking medical assistance. The healing process is closely related to religion because healing requires the sick person to believe in the eficacy of the cure and the healer. Those black people who do not have much faith in western medicine still persist in consulting traditional healers such as diviners and witchdoctors. Only if their methods do not succeed will they consider consulting a western type doctor.

The biggest change stemming from contact with Christianity has been in the religious role of the individual. Traditionally in the tribal religions the individual was of little consequence. The individual acquired meaning in a religious sense largely in terms of the group or tribe. The group provided the framework that explained how the individual was connected with the past and the future, by means of the ancestor cult.

Ancestor worship is a pervasive characteristic of the traditional religions of the blacks. Such religions do not view death as the end of life; instead during death spirits of the ancestors continue to live and take a great interest in the lives of the living. This belief tends to blur the dividing line between life and death, and makes it an event of lesser consequence than is the case in western societies. Because age is the most important determinant of status it has a very interesting effect on the ancestor system. Sex differences become blurred with age to the extent that very old women are treated as if they are men and this lack of differentiation continues into the after-life as well. Because the ancestors are in a way older than the living they are always more senior than them and they are consequently accorded great respect. The ancestors are however not at all alike or equal; each ancestor holds a place on a hierarchy of ancestors that mirrors the status that the same person held during his or her life. At the pinnacle of the ancestral hierarchy is the original chief and immediately below him are all his descendents. It is believed that only the present chief can communicate with these royal ancestors, with the result that whenever there is a problem that concerns the whole tribe then it is the function of the chief to make offerings to the royal ancestors or on behalf of all his people.

233 A Zulu woman diviner (sangoma). The white beads worked into the cotton-bound elongated strands of hair are significant of her profession. Amongst other things, she wears chicken feathers and pieces of buckskin on her head with wire and shell bracelets on her arms.

235▲ 236▼

234

234 A Xhosa woman diviner with a headdress of fur and beadwork and wearing a full-length cape of animal skins. Her costume has many beaded items and has unusually long strands of beads which hang from a heavily beaded necklace.

235 Small clusters of white beads interwoven into the elongated strands of hair signify that this is a young apprentice diviner.

236 A Zulu woman diviner seated on a grass mat inside a "beehive" hut. She wears the characteristic cross-over necklace, which here is made from wood and beads.

The main concern of the ancestors is that their descendants should continue to follow their customs, traditions and lifestyles. It is widely believed that failure by the living to conserve their traditions whether this be conscious or unconscious, will upset the ancestors who in their anger will show their disapproval of these transgressions by bringing misfortune on their descendents. Consequently whenever things go badly, the living will try to find out what it is that they have done wrong. If the living suspect that the ancestors may have something to do with their misfortune then they will consult a diviner to provide them with an answer.

Diviners, or witchdoctors as they are nowadays more commonly referred to, are usually called to their roles by the ancestors. This calling by the ancestors is widely believed to occur when a person becomes diseased with certain characteristic symptoms such as body pains and hallucinations. Success in curing the disease is then taken by the diviners to be a positive sign from the ancestors to indicate that they wish the person to become a diviner. However, before the wishes of the ancestors can be realized the novice diviner first has to pass through a long period of apprenticeship.

Diviners use different methods to diagnose the sources of problems. Perhaps the best known method used is the throwing of bones. In fact these 'bones' also comprise a variety of other objects, such as shells, beads and maybe even bottle tops and dice. Because these objects act as pointers to the cause of the problem, the way in which they fall is of great importance and not considered to be caused by chance. Other divining methods include: a cross questioning session or series of sessions between the diviner and the patient in much the same way as a western doctor questions his patient; the diviner reading the clues in a divining bowl perhaps as a gypsy read the arrangement of tea leaves in a cup; the diviner using a divining rod which would point out possible causes of the problem and by means of ventriloquism, which is when the voices of the ancestors communicate through the diviner. These methods allow the diviner to trace or to smell out the source of the problem and to recommend appropriate action. In most cases an offering to the ancestors may be adequate to restore the balance.

In many cases the cause or causes of the problem do not lie with the disgruntled ancestors, but may be due to some other source such as witchcraft. Witchcraft is caused by people, known as witches, who have the power to use the forces of nature for evil ends. Witches can be people of either sex, although male witches are considered to be more active during the day whereas female witches mainly exercise their witchcraft at night. It is also common for female witches to be unaware of their powers and because they can cause damage unconsciously they are also known as 'unconscious' witches. Witches are usually differentiated from sorcerers in that witches are considered to be born with their evil powers whereas sorcerers have to learn how to deliberately influence the course of nature by magical means to achieve their malign goals.

Witches are believed to meet secretly in special places where they plan their malevolent and anti-social deeds. It is believed that they are assisted in their evil work by so-called familiars, who are often animals such as the hyena, snake, crow and owl. The most famous familiar and in many ways also the most feared especially by women is the thikoloshe, who is believed to have a very hairy body and to have an enormous penis which he carries over his shoulder. It is believed that he is the cause of sexual problems in women and he is consequently to be avoided at all costs. For this reason and for fear of being raped, many women raise their beds on bricks so as to be out of the thikoloshe's reach.

Traditional religion provides two basic ways with which to ward off evil and the misfortunes that befall people. Either a witchdoctor could cast a counter-spell which, hopefully, will be powerful enough to neutralize the harmful spell, or a her-

238 A Bhaca woman diviner wearing the characteristic cross-over of beads and skins. The beaded knob on her head indicates that she is married.

237 A Zulu diviner waiting by the roadside for transport to a meeting of diviners. Inflated goat bladders are often worn by diviners.

239 A Xhosa diviner's accomplice. Her leg bracelets are made from the intertwined roots of a tree and she wears a "doughnut"-shaped grass-covered coil on her head, secured by a beaded chin strap.

240 Lake Fundudzi in Vendaland, legendary home of ancestor spirits and a place where they are venerated.

balist — a specialist in herbal medicines — could be contracted to prepare a medicine to ward off the harm. Medicines are not only used in this negative sense but are also used to ensure the continued fertility of the lands and good harvests. Broadly speaking, medicines are used by the chief and his herbalists, (who have been carefully selected by the chief because they have acquired great prestige and power for their knowledge of medicine and for their previous successes), to promote the solidarity and welfare of the tribe. Medicines are also used for the protection of personal property such as huts and crops against harmful spells and for improving relations between people, particularly those of an amorous nature.

Although there is a widespread belief in an all powerful creator, it is usually of a rather vague nature because the influence and interest of this creative force in the daily lives of the people is of little consequence. The people also believe that there is little they can do to control or influence this creator and there are consequently few rituals or prayers directed at worshipping it. This creator is however important in accounting for the powerful and dangerous forces of nature such as floods, storms and droughts, and oral traditions abound with myths and stories which provide explanations for these natural phenomena.

Nowadays as a result of the fusion of Christian and tribal beliefs, the tribal ancestors are often associated or compared with Christian saints or prophets, whereas the vague creator God of tribal religion has now become a more important and central figure in the new theological system. The most dramatic changes in the religious domain have however stemmed from the social changes which have flowed from the freeing of the individual from his group identity. Nowadays the individual can pray directly to God and is no longer dependant on his chief or on some other intermediary to do so on his or her behalf. Moreover the individual actually believes that his personal prayers will actually be heeded by his God, which is illustrative of a closeness or a proximity between man and his God. This change in the status of the individual does to a large extent symbolize the degree to which the contemporary black person has severed his links with his traditional reference groups.

The so-called Zionist churches which have proliferated amongst both rural and urban blacks have to a great extent incorporated traditional beliefs in a Christian context. The importance in the Zionist churches of dance, singing and music in ritual, and of a strong group identity (which is expressed through a uniform dress), represents a continuity with rituals and religious practices which were important in the tribal setting. The ancestral spirits are also equated with the holy spirit of the Trinity, but unlike the latter, these spirits can possess people and can cause them to become ill. Zionist churches tend to have a mainly female following, very powerful almost messianic leaders, and a preoccupation with healing.

These churches are providing detribalized and disenfranchised people with an avenue within which they can assume responsible roles and a feeling that they are contributing to the welfare of the community.

240

241▲   243▼

242▲   244▼

241 A Tswana diviner throws the bones.
242 A group of Basotho diviners dancing.
243 A male Zulu apprentice diviner.
244 A Swazi girl at a school for diviners.

245 A Pedi diviner reads the "bones".

246 An Ndebele woman diviner.

247 The "bones" of a Zulu diviner.

248 A Zulu diviner with headdress of inflated goat bladders from ritual sacrifices.

248

45▲

246▲   247▼

249 A reed fence around the entrance of the kraal of a Basotho diviner.

250 A diviner with a beaded strap worn across the chin, which is only worn amongst the Basotho. A beaded chin strap is the recognized mark of a Basotho diviner.

251 A Zulu apprentice diviner. The switch in her hand must traditionally be made from the tail of a "wildebees". The switch is a widely recognized hallmark of the diviners' profession.

252 A Shangaan diviner throws the bones for a man seeking his advice.

253 Zulu novice diviners with white clay on their bodies which could denote that they are also initiates. Their dress is mixture of traditional and western, as the large collection of inflated goat bladders on their heads and the decorative slippers testify.

249

250

251▼

252▼

254▲   255▲   256▼

257

257 A member of the Zulu Shembe sect.

258 The uniform of a Zionist sect in the Transkei.

254 A North Sotho priest blesses a congregant.

255 Members of a Zionist church.

256 Zionists on their way to a prayer meeting.

258

259 An early Sunday morning river baptism. These adult baptisms require the candidate for admission to a Zionist church to be at least 16 years of age. Baptism by sprinkling is not recognized, and candidates must enter the water to be completely submerged 3 times — in the name of the Father, Son and the Holy Spirit.

239

260▲

261

260 Mourners at a Pedi funeral.

261 At a Tswana funeral, relatives and friends fill in the grave. They are of the Zionist faith and wear the dress of that religion.

262 Traditional to a Shangaan village is the "Ancestor Tree", under which meetings of importance are held. Horns of cattle which have been ritually slaughtered are nailed to the trunk of the tree, and it is a revered place in the village.

263 The thatch-roofed church, centre of the mission in Giyani, the capital of the Shangaan homeland, Gazankulu.

264 Shangaan patients wait for treatment at the mission hospital.

263

264

CEREMONIES AND FESTIVALS

The context and meaning of traditional festivals and rituals has changed. As most detribalized people no longer physically live off the land, the importance of agricultural festivals in particular have diminished. Formerly there were many festivals relating to the land, such as the "First Fruits", spring ceremonies and rainmaking festivals. Because of the importance of these festivals great care was taken to follow the traditional ritual to ensure the success of the harvest.

These festivals were matters which concerned the whole tribe. Certain people such as the witchdoctors were however more involved in the rituals than others. They would go to great lengths to obtain what they considered to be the proper ingredients for their medicines. These generally included objects associated in some or other way with water or fertility. In some ceremonies pebbles taken from a stream, or frogs, would be used to ensure abundant rain. Some people considered the skin of a very black person to be a particularly potent ingredient, whereas others used different parts of a deceased person's body. More generally these ceremonies revolved around the sacrifice of animals and the sowing of seeds accompanied by certain rituals.

In addition to these agricultural festivals there were numerous others which revolved around matters of importance to the tribe, such as weddings, initiations, burials, victories and the well-being of their leaders. It was customary for the whole tribe to share in the festivities marking any occasion. In this way no body in the group ever felt left out or alone, and the feelings and bonds that tied everyone together were reinforced with each ceremony.

There are three interesting and varied ceremonies with their roots in traditional tribal society which continue to be performed every year, namely the Incwala and Umhlanga ceremonies of the Swazis, and the Zulu Shembe festivities of the followers of Isiah Shembe.

The annual Incwala ceremonies known as the 'small' and 'big' Incwala, which last for two days and a week respectively, revolve around the king because they are aimed at strengthening him for another year of office. The ceremonies are of great importance to the Swazi nation as a whole and are public holidays. The 'big Incwala' ceremony reaches a climax when the naked king straddles and rides a special black bull (which is kept only for its role in this ceremony). The king is symbolically strengthened by drawing power and virility from the bull. In total these Incwala ceremonies last for about three weeks and should be completed before the summer solstice, on 21 December.

The second great Swazi national ceremony is the Umhlanga or "Reed-dance". For the week beforehand all the young girls of the country descend in groups into the river valleys, watched over by local headmen, to gather reeds. The objective of this exercise is for each girl to pluck the best reeds that she can find for the renovation of the Queen Mother's hut and the reed fence which surrounds her homestead. At a huge ceremony at the end of the week the young girls, wearing traditional dress for the special occasion, form a colourful procession and present their tall bundles of reeds to the king. After this the ceremony culminates with dancing before the king and visiting dignatories.

The Zulu Shembe festival is an annual religious event which commemorates the birth of Isiah Shembe, founder of the most influential religious sect amongst the Zulu. Shembe was born in 1870 and died in 1935. He founded the Ama-Nazaretha Church, one of the first independent churches in Southern Africa, in 1922 and became its original leader. The immediate event that led to the formation of this church was a bolt of lightning which struck Shembe but left him unharmed. Before the introduction of Christianity the survival of such an event would have needed an explanation. The diviners would in all likelihood have interpreted this event to be a calling to the survivor to become a diviner. However, due to the spread of Christiani-

Previous page:
265 Young Swazi girls taking part in the 'Umhlanga' or 'Reed Dance' move forward in procession to present the best reeds to the king to refurbish the Queen-mother's hut.

ty at this time, Shembe turned to this ascendant religion for an explanation, instead of becoming a diviner. Inspired by the biblical teachings, Shembe preached that the Zulus were the Nazarites of the Old Testament and that he was their prophet.

Nowadays thousands of Shembe followers converge annually on Isanda which is situated to the north of Durban beyond the town of Verulam. The Shembe festivities continue for a week, culminating on the last day with almost non-stop rhythmic dancing on the hillside near the church. The dancers are in three separate groups — the men and boys, the matrons or unmarried women and the unmarried girls.

266 A group of Zulu men dancing at the Shembe festival.

267 Young Zulu girls beating the traditional drums at the Shembe festival.

268 A priest inaugurates the proceedings for the final day of the festival.

269 Spectators at the dances during the Shembe festival.

270 A group of matrons or married women dressed specially for the Shembe festival, with looped strands of fine beads attached to their traditional headdresss.

267

271

272▲

271 One of the women at the festival wearing the white robe of the Shembe sect.

272 In the last rays of the sun, women seated in the grounds of the church listen to the priest at the end of a long day of celebration.

273 At the Incwala ceremony, the major event of the Swazi year, a warrior wears a cape of teased cowtails, the special dress required for this occasion.

273

274 Ceremonial drums are carried on the heads of these Venda women for use in the national dance.

275 In this national dance, women wear men's waistcoats and trilby hats. The ceremonial drums are also an integral part of the domba or "python dance" performed during the girls initiation.

POLITICAL POWER, ORDER AND JUSTICE

In tribal societies where the behaviour of a person is considered to be more important than what they know, everyone is expected to conform to the proper code of behaviour and etiquette. Everyone is responsible not only for their own behaviour but also for the behaviour of other members in the group. In this way discipline and control are matters which concern the community as a whole as each person in the community is largely responsible for controlling the conduct of the other members. In this way the laws of the tribe are acquired at an early age and young and old people are expected to obey them and behave responsibly. The group does not therefore need any outside organizations or even a special category of person to police the behaviour of society. There are no policemen and no prisons in tribal societies because the worst form of punishment that can be imposed on a person is to be ostrasized from society.

Ostracism is a severe form of punishment in all societies that have a subsistence economy, because the survival of the individual is inextricably linked to the survival of the group as a whole. Being asked to leave the group is therefore almost the same as a death sentence.

There are of course other forms of punishment such as fines, and beatings. Physical mutilation, such as cutting off a finger may be the required form of punishment for serious offences. Punishment is generally based not only on the nature of the crime, but also on the ability of the accused to pay the fine.

Court cases are matters of concern to the whole group and everyone is welcome to attend them. They usually take place whenever required under the shade of a large tree, or in a special courtyard shaded by a tree. All elders can cross-question either of the parties involved in the dispute. These court sessions can proceed for hours until all the parties have had a chance to make their points and complete their cross-examinations. Once it is clear from the evidence who the guilty party is, the elders are called upon to express their verdicts. Ultimately the chief is called upon to pass the final judgement. He proceeds by firstly summing up the main points of the case and then he reviews the evidence. His final verdict, when it is ultimately expressed, is customarily in accordance with the opinions of his councillors and of all present at the hearing. Appeals can be made to the courts of higher chiefs, for there is a hierarchy of courts extending upwards from the level of the ward, to the district and finally to the court with jurisdiction over the whole tribe.

Court cases are usually only held for criminal offences, as these are by their very nature committed against the public or the chief. Most private offences, such as adultery, insults or disobedience, are settled between the two parties themselves. In private cases the parties must agree on a method of settlement which may take the form of material compensation or of giving the injured party a feast. Conciliation is usually achieved during the festivities by the abundance of beer and meat which should be adequate to overcome all the grievances harboured by the injured party.

As almost all the black people in South Africa are now governed from the central government in Pretoria, the sway of traditional tribal law has been greatly diminished. All the traditional powers of the chiefs to adjudicate criminal and statutory law cases have now been transferred to magistrates. By reducing the jurisdiction of the chiefs to the area of petty civil law cases, the stature and position of the chief as in-

276 A Zulu chief wearing a leopardskin cape and a headdress made from the face of a leopard, both exclusively worn by chiefs.

terpreter of the traditional legal system has been irrevocably altered and diminished. Because the powers of the chiefs have been so greatly reduced there has been an accompanying breakdown of discipline. In the towns and cities where the breakdown of discipline has occasionally become critical, certain elders have taken the initiative to form vigilance groups whose task it is to maintain law and order and certain minimum moral standards in accordance with tribal custom.

Traditionally a chief gains legitimacy for his position largely because of his birthright, which stems from him being the eldest son of the chief wife of the former chief. Because a chief is linked by descent to his predecessors, it is his supreme duty to ensure the continuity of tribal traditions and customs. Even with his royal birthright a chief must respect and care for his people if he is to command their allegiance. A chief is expected to act as a father to his people and to guide them in accordance with tribal traditions. He is also expected to provide protection and security for his people, to assist them in times of need and famine and to perform various religious, spiritual and ceremonial duties on their behalf. The relationship between a chief and his people is therefore based on reciprocity, for each is dependant on the other. By withholding their support to the chief, the people can show him their displeasure and dissatisfaction and if the chief still does not rectify matters the people can exercise their ultimate option, which is to move away from his territory. A chief without a people to rule over is of course not worthy of the title. A tribal king is therefore certainly not a despot with unlimited powers. He is expected to consult over all important matters with his councillors who are usually wise elders. It is customary for the chief to make decisions on the basis of complete unanimity, with everyone agreeing on the course of action even if this takes a long time to achieve. The occurrence of a tyrant like Shaka, the Zulu king who held his people in contempt, is therefore an aberration and most certainly not typical of tribal chiefs.

In Southern Africa, only the Swazis and the Basothos escaped being subjugated by the Whites. The Zulus continued to resist White supremacy until the early years of the present century. These three tribes still have their royal ancestors. For example, the king of Swaziland, Sobhuza II was a direct descendant of the first king of the Swazis, Ngwane II, who ruled during the sixteenth century.

King Sobhuza of Swaziland achieved international stature for being both the oldest living monarch and the world's longest ruling king, having ruled for over 60 years on the throne. Just prior to his death, Sobhuza II attempted to achieve the unification of the greater Swazi nation through incorporation into Swaziland of the Ingwavuma region of Zululand in Northern Natal and the Kangwane homeland. The king's pragmatic policies enabled Swaziland to make tremendous strides in the social, economic and education fields, without sacrificing their traditions. The Swazi King was a staunch upholder of traditions and an active participant in many of the traditional ceremonies such as the annual Incwala and Umhlanga ceremonies.

The Basotho King, Moshoeshoe II, is a direct descendant of the founder of the Basotho people, Chief Moshesh. Before dying, Moshesh promised the missionaries from Paris who had been of such great benefit to him and his people, that his descendants would discontinue certain tribal customs which the missionaries found offensive, such as the initiation rites and the institution of polygamy. The influence of these missionaries and of Moshesh's foresight has resulted in Lesotho having the highest literacy rate in Africa apart from South Africa. For this reason subsequent Basotho kings have not strictly adhered to tribal customs and traditions and have been heavily influenced by western values. The current king, for example, has received his university education in England. His role nowadays is mainly of ceremonial importance and his political role is limited to being that of a figurehead.

The Zulu King, Goodwill Zwelithini, can also trace his ancestry back along the royal line of Zulu kings. After the destruction of the Zulu empire in 1876 all the Zulu

277 Three Zulu chiefs taking part in the Shembe religious festival, wearing leopard skins and brightly coloured ostrich plumes.

278 The antlers of a Kudu positioned over the entrance on the roof of this Zulu 'beehive' hut, indicate that it is the hut of a chief. This chief is wearing an ibeshu, which is a skirt made from strips of animal skins. He poses with traditional fighting instruments: a shield made from cowskin, an assegaai and a fighting stick.

kings were stripped of their political power. Although the role of the present king is also largely that of a figurehead, he still symbolizes to his people their link with the glory and grandeur that was the Zulu empire.

The tribal peoples are today divided up into 10 different homelands as follows:

Tribal group	Homeland	Political status
Zulu	Kwa-Zulu	Self Governing 1978
Xhosa	Transkei	Independent 1976
Xhosa	Ciskei	Independent 1981
Venda	Venda	Independent 1981
South Sotho	Basotho Qwa Qwa	Self Governing 1974
North Sotho	Lebowa	Self Governing 1972
Ndebele	Kwa-Ndebele	Self Governing 1981
Swazi	Kangwane	Self Governing 1975
Tsanga-Shangaan	Gazankulu	Self Governing 1972
Tswana	Bophuthatswana	Independent 1977

The physical distribution of these homelands is illustrated in the map below.

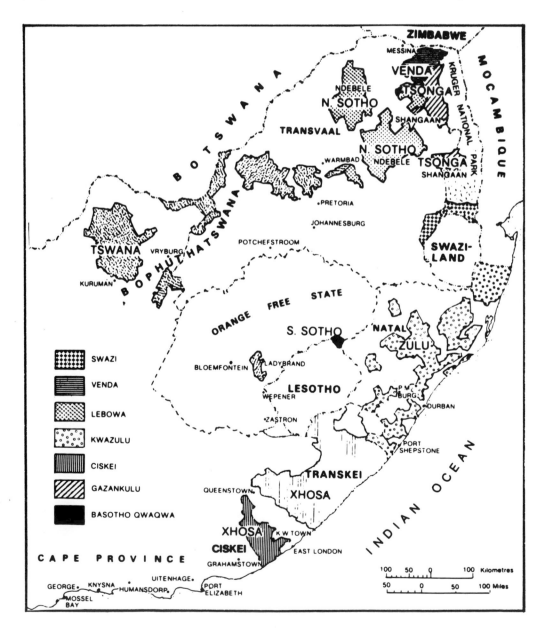

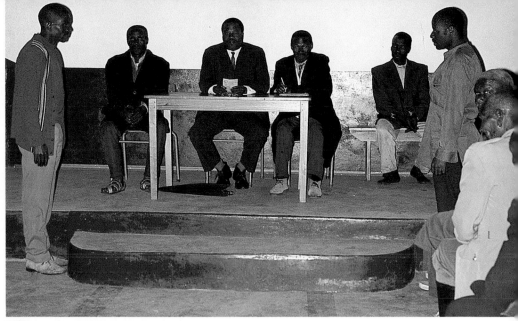

280

279 The first black magistrate appointed in a Northern Sotho area, close to the village of Mujaji.

280 A local chief presides over a court hearing, in a rural area of Zululand.

281 Local Zulu villagers listen attentively to their chief at a Saturday morning court hearing held in a schoolroom.

79▲

281▼

282

282 The distinguished Xhosa chief of a large district, who recently inherited his position on the death of his highly respected father.

283 "Execution Rock", which is on the road to Port St. Johns, in the Transkei. In earlier times political offenders were thrown from the top of this rock to the valley below.

284 The inauguration of a Xhosa chief.

284

283

286

285 A chieftainess kneels in traditional Venda custom at the doorway of her hut.

286 A Venda woman respectfully takes food to the chief in a special basket.

287 A Tswana chief speaks at a "Kgotla", a meeting for adults, under the largest tree in the village.

285▲ **287▼**

288▲

289▲

288 The Zulu King, Goodwill Zwelithini. One of his three wives is a Swazi princess, as it has been customary since the days of Shaka for the Zulu king to marry a Swazi princess, for the maintenance of good political and neighbourly relations.

289 Chief Gatsha Buthelezi, chief minister of KwaZulu. He is also the leader of the Inkatha movement, the biggest political, social and cultural movement in South Africa.

290 King Moshoeshoe II, a direct descendant of Moshesh I who was the founder of the Basotho nation. Here he attends the celebration of his birthday at the national stadium in Maseru. He wears full military uniform to take the salute from the passing military parade.

291 The Houses of Parliament in Gaborone, capital of Botswana.

292 The Tswana Chieftainess of Gopane, in the north west Transvaal. She is also a member of the Bophuthatswana parliament.

293 Brightly dressed delegates attending a seminar for women in Lebowa.

294 The former Rain Queen, known as Mujaji IV, seated on the verandah of her home in the village of "Mujaji", named after the first Rain Queen. These Rain Queens are renowned for their abilities to produce and withhold rain. The time of a Rain Queen's death is shrouded in secrecy and news of it is withheld for one year until a successor is chosen. One is expected when visiting the Mujaji to show respect to her by approaching her homestead on one's hands and knees.

292

293▲ 294▼

EDUCATION

296

297

Scenes from a Shangaan initiation ceremony:

296 One of the girl initiates.

297 Brightly dressed Shangaan girls gather on the final day of the initiation ceremony.

298 Rustling palm leaf skirts are worn by the girl initiates at a certain part of the ceremony. The skirts are made of dried palm leaves which are strung on a very long cord which is twisted several times around the waist, forming a multi-layered skirt.

298

299

299 Family and friends of the initiates watch the afternoon proceedings.

Previous page:
295 An outdoor sewing class at a rural Swazi school.

The values that are now being passed down to the young black children are dramatically different to those treasured in earlier tribal societies. The individual is now all important and this concern for the self finds an expression in the educational fields in that each person must pass his or her own exam. The western education system moreover encourages interpersonal competition so that those who try hardest will get ahead. The knowledge that will enable a person to get ahead in life, although a means to an end, is now the most sought-after goal. Previously in traditional societies, knowledge itself was of lesser consequence than how a person behaved. The education system has therefore been turned upside down and yet some elements of the traditional system continue to survive although in new forms.

The emphasis on correct behaviour persists and survives in the form of a widespread respect for the elderly and in the persistence of values such as loyalty, whether to the family or to an employer; humility and respect to superiors and in maintaining one's dignity even in the most adverse conditions. Since the coming into being of the Soweto generation, many youth are turning against these traditional values which they associate with weakness and acquiescence to domination.

The methods of education have also changed radically. The emphasis has shifted from learning by example and by imitating one's elders in a largely informal setting, to more structured teaching in a more formal setting. The thirst for a western education as a means of getting ahead has resulted in a shift to education that takes place in schools or other institutions of learning.

An outstanding characteristic of traditional tribal education systems is their essentially practical and experiential nature. Because tribal societies do not value knowledge for its own sake there is no need for a person to know any more than society requires of him or her. In tribal education the emphasis is on correct behaviour, that is, behaviour according to tribal custom, rather than on knowledge. It would also not be practicable to take a person out of a productive role in society such as being a herdsman, and to put that person into a dependant and unproductive role in a school, for up to a quarter of that person's life (as is done under western systems of education) because this is a luxury that traditional, subsistence societies cannot afford. In these societies education therefore occurs experientially while the person is working productively on a job. In this manner young girls would learn the proper way of keeping house by participating in this work with their mothers, their contemporaries and their elders.

Young boys on the other hand would go out herding at an early age, often as young as four or five years old, and via direct experience learn everything that needs to be known by herdsmen such as where the sweet grass was to be found, where the water courses were, what predators one found and how to defend the herds against them. As they grew older, they would begin to appreciate the central place of the herd in the social, religious and political life of the tribe. A boy would learn the name of every cow and know the main distinguishing features of each of them in much the same way as a child brought up in a western society learns the names of different automobiles. He would learn that his marriage would be dependent on the herd and also of all the taboos affecting women and the milking of cows. The central economic role of the herd and its by-products as providers of the staple food, of leather for clothes, of utensils and of dung for fuel and the floors of huts, would be passed on to the young herdsman through his daily contact with the herd.

In the traditional way of life, before the initiation ceremony very little formal learning takes place. There are no teachers specially employed for this purpose. Neither are there schools or places set aside specifically for learning. The children therefore learn by experience and by exercising control over their own behaviour. By letting the children assume responsibility at an early age by making them, as members of a group, responsible for the behaviour of their peers, this system of education succeeds where western education often fails. Problems arise in western societies because its youth are put in a dependent situation for a long period which extends well beyond childhood. As a result there is a tendency for many young adults in western society to slide into a situation where they are reluctant to accept any responsibility. This reluctance is accompanied by the occurence of irresponsible behaviour well into adulthood. This situation is exacerbated by the western education systems which pay little attention to correct behaviour or manners, but primarily emphasize the acquisition of a syllabus.

Adolescence is an age of turmoil in everybody's life, because it marks a transitional stage during which a person undergoes both physical and mental changes. Sometimes these changes occur so suddenly that the adolescent can experience great difficulty in adjusting to them. It is common during this stage for adolescents to look with critical eyes at everything that surrounds them including their family and society. Because of all these occurrences many adolscents feel that they are not understood or that they do not quite fit into society, which can result in expressions of rebellion, frustration, and even violence.

Western society does not provide much guidance to the adolescent during this trying stage. The adolescent is largely left alone to piece together the new person that he or she wishes to be. Problems can occur because all the pieces don't always fit too neatly into the puzzle and because parents who should be dispensing advice and understanding are often unable to understand their confused adolescent. In western societies uninterrupted schooling continues until a person is about 18 years of age and this is invariably succeeded by a further period of tertiary study. Through the secondary school stage the young student finds him or herself in a dependant position, sheltered from the demands and responsibilities of adult life as if they are still children, while in fact they are physically mature adults. The dichotomy between these two forces occurs because societal pressures almost require childlike behaviour to be carried forward into adulthood, and in order to cope with this tension anomaly immature or irresponsible behaviour is often resorted to.

Tribal societies have an interesting way of dealing with these forces of change in a person's life. They do this by putting the adolescent through an initiation ceremony. Although these ceremonies vary in detail from one group to the next, they have certain common themes. The most common trait of all initiation ceremonies is the period of seclusion or isolation. During this time while the adolescent is struggling to come to terms with society they are literally taken out of the society to a secluded place where they can rebuild themselves under the guidance of tribal elders and past initiates. In this way they cannot unleash any of their negative or violent feelings on their society.

In isolation away from the prying eyes of society, they are required to build a special initiation hut, wear special clothes and undergo a period of hardship. They are further required to learn a complicated and highly secretive language which is unique to their initiation group only. Failure to master this language in the prescribed period of time and the other lessons of the initiation results in harsh punishment.

Initiation is a period during which the individual is continuously being tested and invariably even the best effort is judged by the supervisors of the initiation to be inadequate and deserving of a beating. The hardships that are endured by male initiates, such as standing in freezing rivers for hours, carrying burning coals and eating stale food are all aimed at teaching the initiates the correct behaviour that their society will expect of them such as being humble and respectful to their elders. While undergoing these hardships they gain an appreciation for the values and comforts of society and can't wait to rejoin their families to take up their new roles.

Not all the initiates succeed in passing through this rigorous period and in some tribes young men actually die. The survivors of the initiation are considered to have proved themselves worthy of rejoining society as an adult. The initiate has passed through a period of transition during which time they have been transformed from children into adults. This initiation ceremony symbolizes the rebirth of a new person because the person that rejoins the society is considered to have a new identity almost as if he has been reborn. To symbolize this break with the past the initiation hut and all the objects used during the initiation ceremony are burned. While the flames consume these artefacts associated with boyhood, the successful graduates stride off into the future and are not permitted to look back. To welcome the new adults back into the group, a feast is held.

Certain groups such as the Pedi and the Lovedu have another interesting institution whereby they deal with this period of transition. Before being initiated they allow the children to build model villages on the outskirts of their village, sufficiently far away from their interfering parents. In these play-play villages the children are given considerable free reign to act out their dreams. The boys can for example enter into relationships with young girls and even "marry" them by undergoing a marriage ceremony conducted by the youngsters; they can elect leaders, rule themselves, hold court cases, go on hunts and so on. Under these idyllic circumstances they can of course enjoy themselves, but conditions generally get increasingly out of control, which is what society expects. Eventually when the behaviour of the children really gets out of hand, the chief calls them to an initiation ceremony which will get them back into line again for once and for all.

This institution is very interesting from an educational point of view, because it allows the children to experiment and to experience things first hand for themselves. The children are given great freedom but are made aware of some constraints on their behaviour by their peers and popular leaders. For example: they are allowed to form intimate relationships but it is a disgrace if these lead to pregnancy. Yet despite these constraints conditions continue to deteriorate and eventually the children are made to appreciate the values and the order that society provides as the only viable alternative to the anarchy that they have created. These ceremonies and institutions give the young tribal person a sense of direction to guide them through a tempestuous period in their lives.

In a carefully planned and programmed manner the secrets and benefits of traditional ways are unfolded to the initiates. Successful integration into society is assured because the initiates are highly motivated to earn the rights and privileges which adulthood bestows on those who pass the test.

Nowadays, except in rural areas, initiation ceremonies are rare and instead most blacks see the acquisition of a mainly western orientated form of knowledge in conventional schools as the main avenue to success in society. The drive to acquire knowledge is strong and competition to gain a university or tertiary qualification is fierce. University education in South Africa still tends to have an ethnic character in the sense that certain universities cater for certain tribal groups, such as for example, the University of the North for the North Sotho, the University of Zululand for the Zulu, and the Universities of Fort Hare and Transkei for the Xhosa. The University of South Africa is, however, open to all races and it has over 10 000 black students and the Medical University of South Africa (MEDUNSA) is open to blacks from any ethnic group.

Tribal and western education, although widely different with regard to content and structure, both recognize the great importance of education in ensuring the survival of values and the crucial role it can play in a better and more secure future.

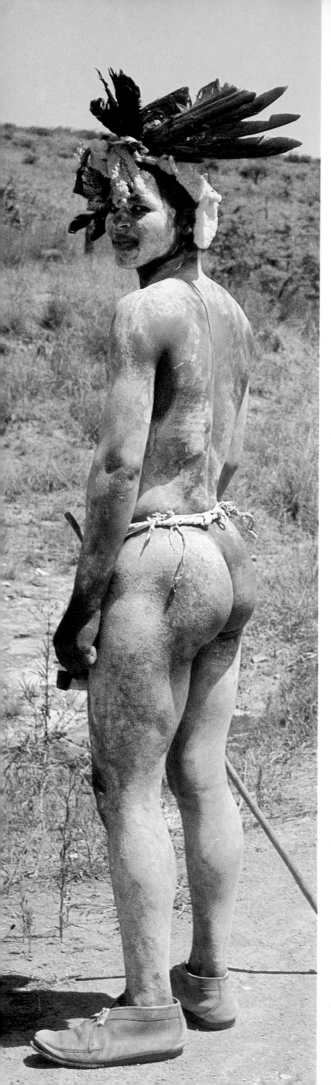

◄**300**   **301**▲

300 A boy initiate in the Ciskei, his face and body covered with white clay and wearing a headdress of sheepskin and owl feathers.

301 Two Xhosa initiation boys.

302 An initiation hut in the Transkei, built in a secluded spot. The initiates live and receive their training in huts like these during a period of about three months. At the end of this period the initiates leave the hut escorted by male relatives who form a line behind them.

302

303 At a given signal the boys drop their blankets to race naked down to the river to wash the white clay from their bodies which has been a mark of their seclusion from the community. The initiates are then anointed with oil and each is given a new blanket to wear.

303

304

305▶

304 The initiation hut is then set alight and the initiates are not allowed to look back at the flames, for this represents their past. The initiates are finally led back to the village by the elders amidst singing and jubilation, to be accepted now as men.

305 & **306** The following day, friends and relatives attend a celebration party where there is much feasting and dancing.

306

307

307 Basotho girl initiates wear straw masks decorated with beads to hide their identities. They also smear their bodies with white clay during this arduous initiation training period between childhood and womanhood.

308 A group of Lovedu girl initiates sing and clap in rhythm at one of the regular nightly meetings, during the three months long initiation.

308

▲ 309

309 Venda girl initiates performing the 'python dance' or Domba, in which all Venda women are required to have taken part in order to attain full status of womanhood.

310 Venda initiates drop to the ground as a sign of respect to the approaching chief. Because in Venda society the chiefs are considered to be synonymous with the land, they are shown great respect by their people.

310

311 At a certain part of the initiation ceremony, Ndebele boy initiates, dressed specially for this occasion, enter the cattle kraal.

312 A procession of initiates in the enormous black city of Soweto, near Johannesburg. In spite of modern urban life some of these tribal traditions are still practiced.

312

313▲

314▲

315▲

316

313 & 315 School children in rural schools in Swaziland.

314 A Venda girl carries her school books home on her head.

316 School children filing back into classes after break.

317 Young children at a nursery school in Soweto.

317

318 Eager Swazi children respond to their teacher in a class held outside the school.

319 The Library of the University of the North near Pietersburg for North Sotho students.

320 Part of the University of Zululand.